INTERNATIONAL DEVELOPMENT IN FOCUS

Spurring Innovation-Led Growth in Argentina

Performance, Policy Response, and the Future

TUGBA GURCANLAR, ALBERTO CRISCUOLO,
DANIEL GOMEZ GAVIRIA, AND
XAVIER CIRERA

WORLD BANK GROUP

1818 H Street NW, Washington, DC 20433
Telephone: 202-473-1000; Internet: www.worldbank.org

1 2 3 4 24 23 22 21

ISBN: 978-1-4648-1689-5
DOI: 10.1596/978-1-4648-1689-5

Cover image: "Endless Innovation," oil on canvas; ©Tugba Gurcanlar. Used with the permission of Tugba Gurcanlar; further permission required for reuse.
Cover design: Debra Naylor / Naylor Design Inc.

Contents

Boxes

Figures

Tables

Preface

The research for this report was completed shortly before the COVID-19 pandemic broke out globally in February 2020, halting and reversing growth and progress on inclusion all around the world. The analysis and findings in the following chapters were derived from data collected and working papers prepared between 2016 and January 2020.

Amid the COVID-19 crisis, the world, including Argentina, is experiencing substantial losses from the recent gains made on shared prosperity and poverty reduction. As Argentina emerges from this historic economic and social crisis, it has the opportunity to strengthen its growth path, and adopt an innovation-based, and more diversified and sustainable growth model. Thus, while the analysis provided in this report was completed prior to the COVID-19 pandemic, its findings, insights, and emphasis on innovation policy and the broader macro- and microeconomic ecosystem required to foster productivity-led growth are even more pertinent today.

The COVID-19 pandemic has underscored the criticality of innovation, as policy makers and private firms rush to adopt or develop technologies to address the health and economic effects of the outbreak. The demand and supply shock exacerbated by the pandemic and subsequent lockdown has highlighted the need for more flexible management and production processes to accommodate social-distance measures and to prepare for what may be very different economic structures in domestic and global markets in the post–COVID-19 era. Going forward, we can expect production processes and service industries to be more automated, digitally integrated, and connected to consumers.

A challenge for policy makers, however, will be that the effects of the pandemic can both bolster and constrain two key dimensions of innovation: invention and diffusion. Regarding invention, the pandemic is boosting research and development on protective equipment, tests, vaccines, and treatments to fight the disease. This is likely to have positive spillovers for broader scientific and medical research in areas such as biotechnology, where Argentina already has considerable strengths. In terms of diffusion, those firms and households that were able to adapt to social distancing with technologies supporting digital communication, conveyance, and commerce are likely to use these technologies after the pandemic and to emerge from it stronger. However, those that do not have access to digital infrastructure or the skills needed for such adaptations will continue to suffer and remain vulnerable. Moreover, the economic contraction, uncertainty, and emergency measures are likely to inhibit investments in invention and diffusion in a variety of other non-COVID areas (such as nonessential services or manufacturing) by cutting resources, softening demand, and dampening expected returns. Policy makers will thus need to find ways to accelerate the technological transformation of their economies while managing these tensions.

At this juncture in its economic history, it is essential that Argentina do more—innovate more, produce more, export more—with less. This would mean making the most of its strengths in areas such as high-end research, and the young entrepreneurial base looking to be unchained. Argentina will have to charter this crisis and beyond with increased policy certainty, and a long-term vision for sustainable growth—all ingredients of an effective innovation policy, as discussed in this report.

While these are very difficult times, Argentina is widely admired for comparative strengths in its natural capital and, in particular, its human capital—strengths upon which it can build with smart policies and targeted investments. A case in point is the positive development announced last summer by MABXIENCE Argentina regarding its partnership with Oxford/Astra Zeneca to manufacture a COVID-19 vaccine for most of the Latin American continent. This company is an extension of one of the innovation programs discussed in this report, a public-private partnership fund that supported 29 such research consortia, many of which successfully linked innovation with a vision for sustained economic growth. MABXIENCE, prior to its involvement in COVID-19 vaccine efforts, also developed and took to market two new cancer drugs. This reduced the price of the existing drugs in the market and increased access by patients, while also resulting in about US$100 million fiscal savings a year for the Argentine government, which would otherwise have imported a more expensive substitute.

This and similar examples of success are results of sustained, transparent, and well-targeted investments in policies and institutions. A stronger innovation policy approach discussed in this report, that builds on such examples, promotes reforms in macroeconomic and fiscal fundamentals, and pushes further the envelope in policy development and implementation at large, will be critical not only in weathering the current storms, but also in taking on more challenges such as the persistent growth divergence and climate change. As World Bank President David Malpass notes in the World Bank's *Global Economic Prospects, January 2021* report, "Making the right investments now is vital both to support the recovery when it is urgently needed and foster resilience. Our response to the pandemic crisis today will shape our common future for years to come. We should seize the opportunity to lay the foundations for a durable, equitable, and sustainable global economy."

Acknowledgments

This report was authored and led by Tugba Gurcanlar (senior economist and private sector specialist, Finance, Competitiveness, and Innovation [FCI] Practice, World Bank), Alberto Criscuolo (senior economist and private sector specialist, FCI), Xavier Cirera (senior economist, FCI), and Daniel Gomez Gaviria (deputy head, National Planning Department in Colombia, and former senior economist, FCI), under the supervision of the FCI regional and central management teams, Latin America and the Caribbean region (LAC) Equitable Growth, Finance and Institutions Practice, LAC chief economist, and LAC vice president offices of the World Bank. The authors would like to thank the government of Argentina, specifically the Ministry of Science, Technology, and Innovation, the Ministry of Production, and the Agencia Nacional de Promoción de la Investigación, el Desarrollo Tecnológico y la Innovación (Agencia I+D+I) and its Project Implementation Unit of the Unleashing Productive Innovation in Argentina program, as well as the Argentinian stakeholders—scientists, researchers, entrepreneurs, businesses, civil society, and academia—that contributed their time, insights, and invaluable cooperation.

The authors benefited from the support and guidance of Jordan Schwartz (country director for Argentina, Paraguay, and Uruguay, World Bank), Jesko S. Hentschel (country director for the Maghreb and Malta, World Bank), Robert R. Talierco (regional director, World Bank), William Maloney (chief economist, World Bank), Martin Rama (chief economist, World Bank), Peter Siegenthaler (program leader, World Bank), Emily Sinnott (former program leader, World Bank), Alfonso Garcia Mora (regional vice president, International Finace Corporation), Denis Medvedev (practice manager, FCI), Zafer Mustafaoglu (practice manager, FCI), Yira Mascaró (practice manager, FCI), Esperanza Lasagabaster (lead economist, World Bank), Cristian Quijada Torres (senior private sector specialist, World Bank), and Cecile Thioro Niang (practice manager, FCI) throughout the preparation and publication of this report. The authors would also like to thank Jaime Frias (senior economist, World Bank), Michael Ehst (senior private sector specialist, World Bank), Steven Dimitriyev (senior private sector development specialist, World Bank), and John Sutton (professor of economics, London School of Economics) for their insightful peer review of the report.

The work builds on a combination of analytical work by the authors and critical inputs received from a series of background papers and impact evaluations created under the umbrella of the project. The authors are especially grateful to Valeria Arza (researcher, National Scientific and Technical Research Council), Anabel Marin (researcher, National Scientific and Technical Research Council), Enrique Carreras (researcher, Center for Transformation), Mariano Pereira (researcher, Interdisciplinary Center for Studies in Science, Technology, and Innovation), Florencia Balestro (expert, Argentine Chamber of Renewable Energies), and Yevgeny Kuznetsov (former senior economist, World Bank) for their contributions to the background papers; to Puja Guha (consultant, World Bank), Elene Allende Letona (consultant, World Bank), Brendan Snow (financial analyst, World Bank), and Elif Nisa Polat (consultant, World Bank) for their crucial analytical and editorial support; to Paula Houser (program assistant, World Bank) for administrative support; and to Cindy A. Fisher (publications officer, World Bank) and Janice Tuten (production editor, World Bank) of the World Bank's Publishing Program.

About the Authors

Xavier Cirera is a senior economist in the Finance, Competitiveness, and Innovation Global Practice at the World Bank and is based in the Brasilia country office. He has more than 15 years of experience in different microeconomic areas of development, including innovation and entrepreneurship policies, productivity, firm-level dynamics, and trade policy. His most recent research work focuses on the measurement of firm-level innovation, the determinants and impacts of innovation, and the relationship between misallocation, productivity, and firm growth. His most recent policy work centers on the evaluation of innovation and entrepreneurship policies, leading the development of the public Expenditure Reviews in science, technology, and innovation implemented in Brazil, Chile, Colombia, and Ukraine. He co-authored *The Innovation Paradox: Developing-Country Capabilities and the Unrealized Promise of Technological Catch-Up* (World Bank 2017) and *A Practitioner's Guide to Innovation Policy: Instruments to Build Firm Capabilities and Accelerate Technological Catch-Up in Developing Countries* (World Bank 2020). Before joining the World Bank, he was a research fellow at the Institute of Development Studies at the University of Sussex. He holds a PhD in economics from the University of Sussex.

Alberto Criscuolo is a senior economist at the World Bank with more than 18 years of experience in development economics, focusing primarily on regional development, trade, competitiveness, and innovation in emerging markets. In his various roles at the World Bank Group, Alberto designed and supervised lending and advisory programs to promote innovation, firm growth, and diversification across various regions, including Eastern Europe and Central Asia (ECA), Latin America and the Caribbean (LAC), and South Asia. He recently rejoined the ECA team of the Finance, Competitiveness, and Innovation Global Practice to lead the portfolio on regional integration and global value chain upgrading in the Western Balkans. While on the LAC team, he led the program on innovation, global value chains, and investment climate reform in Argentina, Chile, Peru, Uruguay, and Central America. Alberto holds an MCP in international development and regional planning from Massachusetts Institute of Technology and a BA in economics from the University Federico II of Naples.

Daniel Gomez Gaviria is deputy director at the National Planning Department in Colombia. Previously, he was a senior economist in the Finance, Competitiveness, and Innovation (FCI) Global Practice on the Latin America and the Caribbean region team. Based in Buenos Aires, he was the focal point for FCI work in the Southern Cone (Argentina, Paraguay, and Uruguay). Daniel has experience in competitiveness; productive development policy; science, technology, and innovation policies; trade policy; and competition policy. Before joining the World Bank Group, he was the head of Competitiveness Research at the World Economic Forum (WEF), where he led the production of the *Global Competitiveness Report*. He designed and led country engagement strategies including competitiveness labs and workshops in Argentina, Brazil, Colombia, El Salvador, Guatemala, Mexico, and Peru. He also led research on technological diffusion and productive transformation resulting in a new benchmarking tool on country readiness for future production. Before that, Daniel was advisor to the Minister of Trade, Industry, and Tourism of Colombia, where he led policy work on competitiveness and productive development policy; a researcher with Fedesarrollo, the main public policy think tank in Colombia; and an adjunct professor of economics at Universidad de los Andes and Universidad Javeriana in Bogotá. He holds a PhD in business economics with specializations in international trade and industrial organization and an MBA from the Booth School of Business at the University of Chicago, and an MSC in banking and finance and a BA in economics from HEC University of Lausanne.

Tugba Gurcanlar is a senior economist and senior private sector specialist in the Finance, Competitiveness, and Innovation Global Practice at the World Bank. She has more than 15 years of experience in development economics policy and operations, with a primary focus on competitiveness, trade, finance, and innovation in emerging and developing markets. In her various roles at the World Bank Group, Tugba designed, supervised, and led investment operations and other lending and analytical programs to promote private sector growth and diversification to advance shared prosperity in client countries. She has worked in more than 25 countries across income groups and regions in East Asia and Pacific, Europe and Central Asia, South Asia, Sub-Saharan Africa, and, most recently, Latin America and the Caribbean. She has written about the underlying policy issues for venues including the World Economic Forum and *McKinsey Quarterly* and for International Monetary Fund and World Bank internal publications. In 2018, Tugba was one of the first recipients of WBG-IFC top 30 individuals award for her work on maximizing finance for development and creating markets in developing countries. In her current role, among others, Tugba leads the World Bank's program on innovation and its contribution to growth in Argentina. Her previous work in the Research, Finance, and Trade Departments focused on global competitiveness, South-South banking, international trade corridors, and integration of emerging markets into global supply chains. Tugba holds a BA from Connecticut College, an MPP from Duke University, and an MBA from Columbia University.

Overview

A new growth model based on innovation and productivity would enable Argentina to increase economic stability and achieve stronger shared prosperity. Argentina can escape the recurrent boom-and-bust cycles with an innovation-driven economy that, in addition to factor accumulation, fuels constant productivity growth. Such a growth model would derive momentum from Argentina's strengths in human capital, research, and firm-level capabilities, which are less susceptible to external shocks and contribute to inclusive growth, as well as economic resilience, by providing the country with a stronger buffer at times of uncertainty. Achieving this stability requires a long-term vision and a policy framework that builds a sustainable national innovation system with a view to diversifying and strengthening Argentina's sources of growth.

A different economic trajectory is possible with a more efficient and strategic use of Argentine assets in human capital and high-end research and their closer alignment with firm-level capabilities and productivity growth. The recurrent crises and ensuing economic downturns paint a bleak picture for Argentina, especially for Argentines who suffer the negative repercussions on their wages, purchasing power, employment, and overall standard of living. In spite of the economic volatility of the past few decades, Argentina has been able to develop important pockets of success in human capital, high-end research, and frontier productive sectors, all of which should be better exploited and strengthened through public-private partnerships, investments, and an enabling business environment. Argentina has the highest share of researchers per capita in Latin America and some of the top research organizations in the world. Between 2004 and 2016, Argentina expanded its research base by 36 percent (to 3 researchers per 1,000 employees)—the highest increase in the region. In 2019 it ranked among the top 30 countries in the world in terms of the excellence of its research organizations—in both cases significantly ahead of regional comparators such as Chile and Mexico. Meanwhile, knowledge-intensive sectors such as biotechnology, nanotechnology, and software, while still small, emerged for the first time or grew substantially; in some business segments, Argentina became globally competitive. Today, Argentina is the world's third biggest producer of biotech crops, after the United States and Brazil, and one of the most prolific producers of new technologies in this sector.

The growing strengths in some of the factors serving as innovation inputs were also paralleled by progress on the policy front, which increased the focus on industry links and firm-level productivity. Traditionally, Argentine "innovation policy" focused almost exclusively on academic sciences and education. In the past decade, however, the policy mix supporting science, technology, and innovation (STI) has become more balanced, with noteworthy changes including the promotion and realignment of incentives in public-private partnerships. These changes were underpinned by the creation of institutions such as the Ministry of Science, Technology, and Productive Innovation (MINCyT), National Agency for the Promotion of Science and Technology (Agencia I+D+I), and a new technology transfer unit in the National Scientific and Technical Research Council (CONICET), which started in 2007, as well as by an increased emphasis by the Ministry of Production on supporting firm-level productivity. These efforts helped to improve Argentina's international rankings on the World Economic Forum's Innovation Index and the quality of research institutions (which moved Argentina from 98th to 56th place and from 90th to 26th place, respectively, between 2007 and 2019).

Despite these improvements, innovation made only a limited contribution to economic growth. In Argentina, innovation has a positive impact on productivity and produces returns, but these impacts are limited and heterogeneous. Argentina's innovation outputs in terms of new products, processes, and businesses continue to lag significantly behind both regional and structural peers and are not commensurate with the quality of some of its inputs. Thus, the Argentine "knowledge function"—the ability to transform knowledge into innovations taken to market—displays inefficiencies and is unable to transform innovation inputs into significant growth.

Gaps across the innovation function can explain some of these inefficiencies. While Argentina's gross expenditure on research and development (R&D) is low, but similar to that of its regional peers, private sector R&D investments are especially low, falling 21 percent in value between 2007 and 2016. In Argentina, the business share of gross R&D expenditure is the lowest among its regional and structural comparators (17 percent as opposed to as high as 50 percent for Turkey). Other channels of knowledge transfer are similarly lagging: only 8 percent of businesses use technology licensed by foreign firms and 44 percent of firms invest in fixed assets. Knowledge and research capacity are concentrated in the public sector and far from the market and commercialization.

Limited firm-level capabilities, such as managerial practices, inadequate skills, and limited links between science and industry also affect firms' absorptive capacity and depress the returns to innovation. Argentina lags in the quality of managerial practices, decreasing the efficiency of R&D spending. The share of graduates in the science, technology, engineering, and mathematics (STEM) fields is the second lowest among countries in the Organisation for Economic Co-operation and Development, which contributes to a low level of absorptive capacity for technology adoption. Argentina also has the lowest score for innovation links between science and industry among its regional and structural peers, as measured by the World Economic Forum's innovation index (2018).

Meanwhile, macroeconomic imbalances and the high cost of finance reduce the incentives to invest in innovation. Credit to the private sector in Argentina is the lowest in Latin America and the Caribbean, at 14 percent, which is particularly low relative to the regional average of 44 percent. Combined with nascency and shallowness of venture and private equity markets and interest rates that historically average 30 percent, financing for innovation and entrepreneurship is especially hindered. Addressing these imbalances, improving the business environment, strengthening the competition landscape, and reducing uncertainty at-large will all be key to propelling innovation in Argentina.

Against this backdrop, shortcomings, inconsistencies, and frequent shifts in the policy mix also contribute to the absence of innovation impact on the economy. While progress has been made in the past decade, the STI policy mix still fails to respond to the entire range of market failures that underpin innovation's subpar performance. For example, according to a recent public expenditure review, the 2018–19 policy mix overwhelmingly favored tax incentives, which are tailored to compensate for externalities and tend to be procyclical; they address only one type of innovation problem and are unlikely to be the most appropriate policy instrument in times of economic uncertainty. Moreover, economic volatility leaves the government limited space for policy response and offsets further policy instability, thereby encroaching on the progress achieved in the recent decade. The 2017–18 budget realignment affected STI policies disproportionately, reducing them from 1.5 percent of total spending in 2015 to 1.1 percent in 2018; growth-oriented policies for export promotion and entrepreneurship were reduced the most. The STI policy mix also suffered from frequent changes in objectives and institutional arrangements during this time. These changes can inadvertently undermine the overall goal of productive innovation and diversification.

While fiscal adjustments introduce resource constraints, they also can motivate efficiency improvements and strategic realignment of policies for higher and sustained returns from Argentina's innovation inputs. Although most innovation policies are unable to address the hindrance that macro volatility poses to both innovation outcomes and firm decisions to invest in innovation, policy interventions can still focus on building firm capabilities and links that promote dynamism, productive developments, and exports. Furthermore, some of the programs focusing on innovation show positive returns, with notable contributions to fiscal savings. For example, a public-private partnership enabled two biosimilar cancer drugs to be taken to market, resulting in annual cost savings of more than US$100 million for the health care system. Impact evaluations also find increases in the creation of technology-based firms (30 percent more likely) and the ability to obtain private financing (12.8 percent higher). Meanwhile, resource constraints make it ever more important for Argentina to focus on monitoring and evaluation—an area that has been especially lacking in the STI policy mix. This will also help to streamline and consolidate the policy mix where appropriate—a recent STI public expenditure review shows that a few policy instruments absorb most of the budget, while more than 200 instruments are identified in this space,[1] making it likely that the remaining instruments are underfunded or surviving by inertia. Improved collection of results, reporting and transparency of the underlying data, enhanced coordination between different line agencies, and better identification of strengths, assets, and bottlenecks will ensure that policy gains are sustained and the impact of policy response is optimized against costs.

Overall, Argentina needs to develop a long-term strategy, increase institutional predictability and policy certainty, improve the effectiveness of policy responses, and prioritize innovation as a tool for growth. Given Argentina's knowledge assets in terms of human capital and research, neglecting firms' absorptive capacity and links between research and industry essentially leaves money on the table for the overall economy. Policy interventions focused on these areas, with an enhanced emphasis on monitoring and evaluation, instruments that minimize moral hazard and improve targeting, and sustained progress in developing the capacity of the institutions that support the innovation environment can help to achieve better and more sustainable growth outcomes. These interventions will need to be accompanied by measures that continue to improve the ease of doing business in the country, so that the eventual impact on firm-level productivity can take hold. Similarly, stronger regional innovation policies will also be key to maximizing efficiency gains and impact. Recent empirical research shows that innovation returns vary widely between sectors and regions in Argentina, underscoring the need for regional policies that support entrepreneurs by addressing province-specific market failures and strengthening nationwide support systems. All in all, improving innovation's contribution to diversifying Argentina's sources of growth requires a sustained strategy that is focused on medium- to long-term goals with a stable roadmap of regional and national policies tailored closely to address gaps and exploit opportunities, which maximize the economic and social returns for the country.

In this report, we review the innovation performance, identify gaps and strengths, discuss the appropriateness of the policy response, examine regional differences in economic performance, and review impact evaluations of recent initiatives that focused on industry and science links and knowledge-based entrepreneurship to provide guidance for the future of innovation policy in Argentina.

NOTE

1. The top five instruments in the Ministry of Production, Ministry of Agribusiness, and MINCyT account for 85 percent, 83 percent, and 75 percent of the budget, respectively.

Abbreviations

Agencia I+D+I	National Agency for the Promotion of Science and Technology
ANR TEC	Nonreimbursable Grants for Technology Projects (Aportes No Reembolsables Technología)
CAME	Argentine Confederation of Medium-Sized Enterprises
CONICET	National Scientific and Technical Research Council (Consejo Nacional de Investigaciones Científicas y Técnicas)
DD	difference in difference
EEAOC	Experimental Agroindustrial Station (Estacion Experimental Agroindustrial Obispo Colombres)
EMPRETECNO	Argentine fund supporting technology-based entrepreneurship
ENDEI	National Survey of Employment Dynamics and Innovation
FONARSEC	National Agency for Scientific and Technological Promotion
FONCyT	Fund for Scientific and Technological Research
FONDEAR	Argentine Economic Development Fund
FONSOFT	Software Industry Promotion Trust Fund
FONTAR	Argentine Technological Fund
FONTEC	Argentine Technological Entrepreneurship Fund
FSAT	sectoral funds
GDP	gross domestic product
GERD	gross expenditure on research and development
GII	Global Innovation Index
ICT	information and communication technology
M&E	monitoring and evaluation
MINCyT	Ministry of Science, Technology, and Productive Innovation
MoP	Ministry of Production
NIS	national innovation system

OECD	Organisation for Economic Co-operation and Development
PER	public expenditure review
PPP	purchasing power parity
PSM	propensity score matching
R&D	research and development
SDA	Schumpeterian Development Agency
SME	small and medium enterprise
STEM	science, technology, engineering, and mathematics
STI	science, technology, and innovation
TFP	total factor productivity

1 Introduction

Reinforcing Argentina's strengths in innovation has the potential to result in long term, sustainable growth and deliver shared prosperity, at the same time addressing challenges such as recovery from the COVID-19 crisis, climate change, and persistent growth divergence. Empirical cross-country studies demonstrate that productivity improvements account for half of gross domestic product (GDP) growth (Easterly and Levine 2001). Innovation is a key component of such productivity improvements; and thus transitioning Argentina's growth model toward innovation-fueled, multiple engines of growth will be critical to escaping the recurrent boom and bust cycles that have plagued the economy. This transition requires a holistic approach to strengthen Argentina's innovation system by tackling multiple factors that impact Argentina's knowledge function, and its ability to improve firm-level productivity and diversification outcomes.

LONG-TERM GROWTH, PRODUCTIVITY, AND INNOVATION

Innovation is an important component of productivity and a significant contributor to growth, underpinning dynamism in successful economies. Innovation is the essence of creative destruction that has come to characterize transformational growth (Schumpeter 2008 [c1934]) across the world. Andrews and Criscuolo (2013) identify three stages in the innovation process: new ideas and technologies, their commercialization, and the dynamic benefits that occur through changes in the reallocation of resources to growing firms. They find that, when combined, these three stages can account for as much as half of economic growth, depending on each country's level of economic development and phase of the economic cycle.

A growing body of evidence, including in Argentina, shows that increased innovation activity has a measurable, positive impact on productivity and economic growth. Similar to global findings (Mohnen and Hall 2013), recent empirical estimates from Argentina based on the second National Survey of Employment Dynamics and Innovation (ENDEI) results for 2,630 firms and 27 manufacturing sectors (2014–16) find that innovation has a positive impact on productivity; Argentine firms that engage in innovative activities achieve higher total factor productivity than those that do not (Galiani, Jaitman, and Soares 2019).

Innovation-fueled growth is also key to escaping the middle-income trap. Seminal studies on income divergence among countries suggest that adoption of technology and investment in innovation play important roles in a country's ability to move to higher income levels. Comin and colleagues, for example, argue that differences in the rate of adoption of new technologies drive the magnitude of the "Great Divergence" of incomes between high-income and low- and middle-income economies (Comin and Ferrer 2013; Comin and Hobijn 2004). Maloney and Valencia Caicedo (2017) further suggest that the ability to identify, absorb, and adopt technologies, as represented by the number of engineers per capita, is a key part of the divergence story (figure 1.1). Accordingly, they show that a country's capability for innovation in the 1900s drives their income levels today.

Figure 1.1, panel a, compares innovation capabilities across a number of countries in terms of the number of engineers per 100,000 male workers relative to GDP per capita in 1900. Figure 1.1, panel b, demonstrates the result of innovation investments by showing the change in labor productivity from innovation relative to GDP per capita in 2017 across several countries.

Despite changes in the dynamics of global growth, investments in innovation continue to produce significant dividends for economies around the world, with higher returns for countries farther from the technological frontier. Recent studies demonstrate continued high returns to investments in research and development (R&D) even in high-income economies. For example, Bloom, Schankerman, and Van Reenen (2013) and Lucking, Bloom, and Van Reenen (2017) find social returns of between 55.0 percent and 57.7 percent and private returns of between 13.6 percent and 20.7 percent. More important, however, and in line with Schumpeterian catch-up theory, Griffith, Redding, and Van Reenen (2004) find that the returns to R&D in the Organisation for Economic Co-operation and Development are higher for countries farther from the technological frontier than for countries closer to it. Extrapolating from their results implies that the returns to R&D could easily be 200 percent to 300 percent for low- and middle-income economies even farther from the frontier.

FIGURE 1.1

Capability for and returns from innovation in selected countries, by GDP per capita

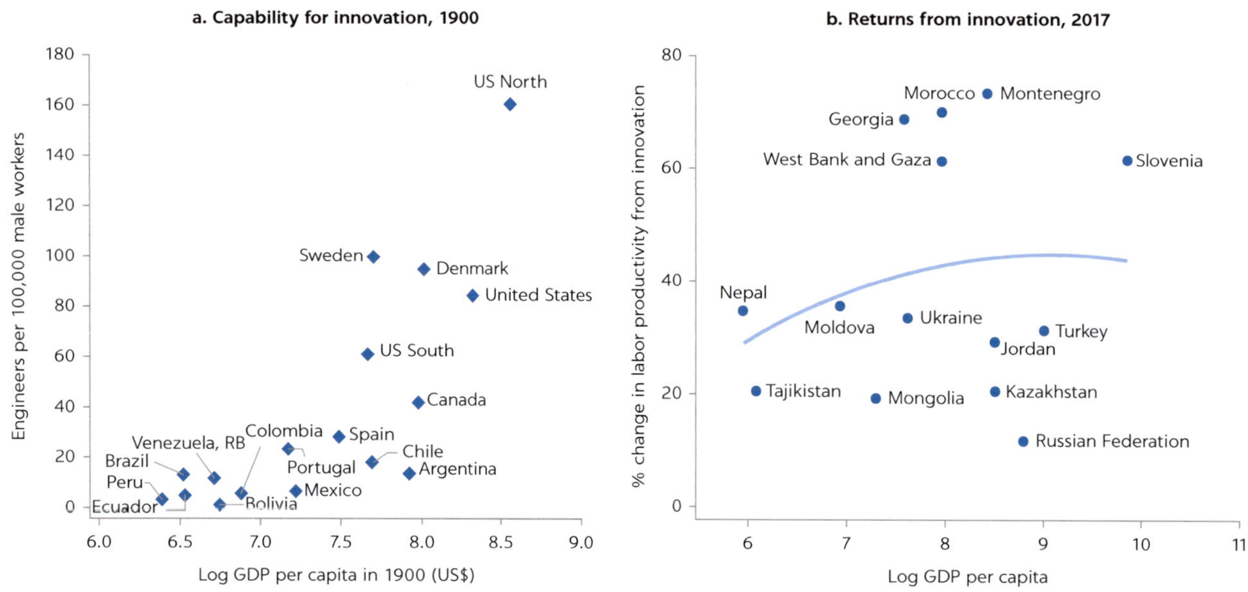

Source: Maloney and Valencia Caicedo 2017.

However, returns are not always the highest in the poorest countries due to three sets of factors: (a) absence of macro and micro complementarities, (b) firm-level weaknesses, and (c) institutional and policy challenges. While many firms in low- and middle-income countries achieve positive returns from investing in innovation activities, these returns are often below the large gains predicted by the Schumpeterian catch-up theory (Cirera and Maloney 2017). This underinvestment and underperformance in innovation, despite the large expected gains, can be explained by three groups of factors: (a) a lack of complementarities needed to realize high potential returns (that is, macroeconomic stability and trade openness, among others); (b) missing firm capabilities, which are required for firms to undertake innovation and commercialize it (that is, managerial qualities); and (c) weaknesses in government capabilities for implementing effective innovation policies (Cirera and Maloney 2017). Indeed, using country-level panel data, Goñi and Maloney (2017) estimate the relationship between returns to R&D and country income; consistent with earlier studies (Griffith, Redding, and Van Reenen 2004), they find that the rate of return to R&D investment increases with distance from the frontier only up to high upper-middle-income levels. Similarly, Cirera and Maloney (2017) present estimates of the rate of return to both innovation activities and R&D intensity at the country level based on World Bank Enterprise Surveys; their analysis shows that, when significant, returns are positive and often very high for those few firms that invest in R&D, but that, overall, they are still not as high as those found in high-income economies.

These findings also help to explain Argentina's underinvestment in innovation, especially in the private sector, and its lagging productivity and diversification outcomes. In Argentina, innovation has a significant impact on productivity and produces returns, but these returns are limited and heterogeneous (Arza et al. 2020). Accordingly, in the rest of this report, we discuss Argentina's innovation performance at the aggregate level, starting with the limited impact on productivity and growth observed, benchmarking the innovation inputs and outputs that contribute to these outcomes, and discussing the factors that explain the performance. We then explore in more detail the coherence and adequacy of recent policy responses to the challenges identified across the innovation function and the factors driving these responses.

CONCEPTUAL FRAMEWORK AND STRUCTURE OF THE REPORT

In subsequent chapters, we review the innovation ecosystem in Argentina across innovation inputs and outputs, institutional capabilities, and macro- and firm-level factors that influence the country's innovation outcomes and impact.

In chapter 2, we use an "innovation function analysis" and benchmark Argentina's performance across a range of both innovation inputs, such as human capital, public and private R&D, and managerial practices, and innovation outputs, such as patents and new businesses, products, and processes. Figure 1.2 describes the innovation function, outlining the relationship between innovation inputs and knowledge activities, innovation outputs and outcomes, and their impact in terms of firm growth, productivity growth, and economic diversification.

The innovation function analysis addresses some of the limitations of measures that focus mainly on performance in science and research and aligns

FIGURE 1.2
Innovation function

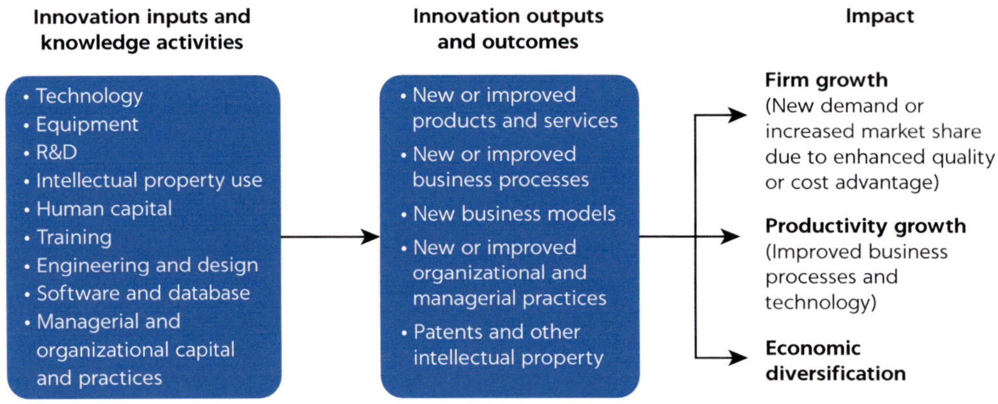

Source: Cirera and Maloney 2017.
Note: R&D = research and development.

innovation more closely with productivity and economic growth. It also enables identification of the relative weaknesses and strengths in the broader ecosystem, thereby supporting policy making by providing more concrete ways to identify and address gaps and opportunities. This framework builds on the Schumpeterian view of innovation, which entails both more popular interpretations, such as invention, patenting, or the generation of disruptive technologies, as well as the more incremental implementation of ideas and knowledge to improve the firm. Consequently, in this report, measures of innovation go beyond "percentage of GDP spending in R&D" or "number of academic papers produced and cited" and "PhDs trained." Here, innovation is defined more broadly as a range of applications, such as (a) introduction of new or upgraded products, (b) use of a new process or technology in an industry, (c) discovery of a new market, (d) discovery of new sources of inputs, and (e) changes in industrial organization.

Accordingly, in chapter 2 we benchmark the expected impact of the innovation function—firm growth, productivity growth, and economic diversification—using recent literature and global databases and then highlight some of the weaknesses and relative strengths in innovation inputs and outputs, using the same set of sources as well as relevant global rankings and analyzing the literature dealing with these constituents. We then unpack the underpinning drivers of underperformance in the three groups of factors that have been determinants of low returns and investment in low- and middle-income countries at-large. Hence, we first review macro complementarities based on recent trends in Argentina and analyze how these are likely contributing to subpar outcomes. We then discuss firm-level capabilities, based both on recent global analysis as well as on new empirical evidence for Argentina, and note the challenges presented by inadequate policy response.

The analysis uses the most recent empirical research that moves beyond a neoclassical simplification of a firm with clear foresight to the technology frontier and only affected by a set of well-identified market failures. Indeed, the global evidence establishes that a confluence of factors across macro and micro foundations, gaps in policy response, and weaknesses in firm-level capabilities underpin innovation's limited contributions to growth outcomes in the world. For this reason, we review the macro-level complementarities that affect firms' ability to act on market signals and invest in innovation based on expected returns as well as firm-level capabilities (production, technological adoption, and invention) that influence the absorptive capacity gained from investments in innovation. We use this framework to provide a balanced understanding of macro- and micro-level factors that affect the impact and outcomes of innovation and posit that the ability of firms to introduce innovation eventually also depends on their capabilities, “which can be defined as those elements of the production process that cannot be bought ‘off the shelf’ on the market like a normal input and hence must be learned and accumulated by the firm” (Sutton 2012).[1] The importance of these intangible firm-level capabilities is increasingly evident in the fast-changing world of disruptive technologies and high-growth entrepreneurs. As Hal Varian, Google chief economist, puts it, future success will belong to those businesses that “seek to be a scarce complement to increasingly abundant inputs” (Benzell and Brynjolfsson 2019, 2).

In chapter 3, we discuss the policy response in greater detail based on a light public expenditure review (PER) of the science, technology, and innovation (STI) policies conducted for this report.

In chapter 4, we provide some insights from impact evaluations of recent policy initiatives that endeavored to focus more closely on the weaknesses and gaps across the innovation function in Argentina. Table 1.1 maps the methodology or conceptual framework and associated data sources for each chapter of this report.

TABLE 1.1 **Methodology and data sources**

CHAPTER	METHODOLOGY OR CONCEPTUAL FRAMEWORK	DATA SOURCES
2: Innovation Performance	Innovation function analysis (Cirera and Maloney 2017). The chapter benchmarks Argentina’s performance across the inputs, outputs, and expected impact of innovation relative to the country’s structural and regional peers and discusses the gaps based on findings from the global literature.	OECD database on STI; World Bank, World Development Indicators and Enterprise Surveys; Harvard’s Atlas of Economic Complexity; COMTRADE; Global Entrepreneurship Monitor; Global Innovation Index; Argentina’s ENDEI; UNESCO data; global literature on determinants of innovation
3: Public Expenditure Review of Innovation Policies in Argentina	Analysis of the current STI policy portfolio in Argentina, based on a light public expenditure review of the corresponding budgets for 2017–18. The analysis follows the methodology described in Correa (2014). The chapter (a) assesses the magnitude, appropriateness, and coherence of the STI system in Argentina by comparing Argentina’s innovation policy priorities with the current set of STI policy instruments and (b) analyzes three typologies of instruments that fall under the category “transfers to firms”: forgone fiscal revenue due to tax incentives; direct transfers to firms, including grants and matching grants; and indirect transfers to firms, including advisory support and subsidized access to credit. The PER analysis uses these data to evaluate the coherence between policy priorities and the actual policy portfolio and to assess internal consistency within the policy mix to come up with recommendations. The PER focuses on 216 active instruments, constituting a fairly comprehensive representation of the current policy mix, and analyzes the number of policy instruments across different themes and tools as well as the total value of spending. Of the 216 active instruments, budget data are available for only 103 instruments. A full description of the methodology used is provided in appendixes C and D.	The database is constructed using the Registro de Subsidios e Incentivos created by the Ministry of Production and lists all available STI instruments (World Bank 2019b).

continued

TABLE 1.1 *continued*

CHAPTER	METHODOLOGY OR CONCEPTUAL FRAMEWORK	DATA SOURCES
4: Insights from Recent Initiatives Supporting Public-Private Partnerships and Knowledge-Based Entrepreneurship	Impact evaluation of the EMPRETECNO initiative (World Bank 2019a): quasi-experimental evaluation design with a difference-in-difference model combined with propensity score matching that estimates a program's impact on the likelihood of business creation, the survival rates of new businesses, and the likelihood of crowding in private financing	The database for the evaluation combines two sources of information: (a) the administrative records of FONARSEC, including both applicants and program beneficiaries, and (b) a database that provides information on the EMPRETECNO applicants both before and after the program. These data are used to construct panel data for 209 entrepreneur teams and 418 observations.
	Impact evaluation of FONARSEC: difference-in-difference model combined with propensity score matching of the estimated impact of firms' participation in FSAT (public-private partnerships in innovation support by FONARSEC)	To build the database, the list of firms that integrate both a treatment and a comparison group are merged with the innovation survey of FONTAR. The result of the integration is a balanced set of panel data for 111 firms with 222 observations. Among them, 34 firms correspond to the treatment group and the remaining 77 correspond to the control group. The panel data include information at two points in time: before and after the program.
	Qualitative and financial evaluations of EMPRETECNO and FONARSEC	Evaluations were conducted based on field visits and monitoring and evaluation data available from the Unleashing Productive Innovation in Argentina Program (administered by MINCyT and the World Bank).

Source: World Bank.
Note: COMTRADE = United Nations International Trade Statistics Database; EMPRETECNO = Argentine fund supporting technology-based entrepreneurship; FONARSEC = Argentine Sectoral Fund; FONTAR = Argentine Technological Fund; INDEC = National Institute of Statistics and Censuses; MINCyT = Ministry of Science, Technology, and Innovation; OECD = Organisation for Economic Co-operation and Development; PER = public expenditure review; STI = science, technology, and innovation; UNESCO = United Nations Educational, Scientific, and Cultural Organization.

In chapter 5, we summarize the findings and provide some recommendations for Argentina to consider.

NOTE

1. These capabilities can range from basic organizational skills, to logistical abilities (see Syverson 2011), to planning routines and systems of human resource management.

REFERENCES

Andrews, Dan, and Chiara Criscuolo. 2013. "Knowledge-Based Capital, Innovation, and Resource Allocation." OECD Economics Department Working Paper 1046, Organisation for Economic Co-operation and Development Publishing, Paris.

Arza, Valeria, Xavier Cirera, Augustina Colonna, and Emanuel López. 2020. "Explaining Differences in the Returns to R&D in Argentina." Policy Research Working Paper 9219, World Bank, Washington, DC.

Benzell, Seth G., and Erik Brynjolfsson. 2019. "Digital Abundance and Scarce Genius: Implications for Wages, Interest Rates, and Growth." NBER Working Paper 25585, National Bureau of Economic Research, Cambridge, MA.

Bloom, Nick, Mark Schankerman, and John Van Reenen. 2013. "Identifying Technology Spillovers and Product Market Rivalry." *Econometrica* 81 (4): 1347–93.

Cirera, Xavier, and William F. Maloney. 2017. *The Innovation Paradox*. Washington, DC: World Bank.

Comin, Diego, and Martí Mestieri Ferrer. 2013. "If Technology Has Arrived Everywhere, Why Has Income Diverged?" NBER Working Paper 19010, National Bureau of Economic Research, Cambridge, MA.

Comin, Diego, and Bart Hobijn. 2004. "Cross-Country Technology Adoption: Making the Theories Face the Facts." *Journal of Monetary Economics* 51 (1): 39–83.

Correa, Paulo. 2014. "Public Expenditure Reviews in Science, Technology, and Innovation: A Guidance Note." World Bank, Washington, DC.

Easterly, William, and Ross Levine. 2001. "What Have We Learned from a Decade of Empirical Research on Growth? It's Not Factor Accumulation: Stylized Facts and Growth Models." *The World Bank Economic Review* 15 (2): 177–219.

Galiani, Sabastian, Laura Jaitman, and Ricardo Soares, eds. 2019. "Special Issue: 50 Years of the Economics of Crime." *Journal of Economic Behavior and Organization* 159 (March): 1–662.

Goñi, Edwin, and William F. Maloney. 2017. "Why Don't Poor Countries Do R&D? Varying Rates of Factor Returns across the Development Process." *European Economic Review* 94 (C): 126–47.

Griffith, Rachel, Stephen Redding, and John Van Reenen. 2004. "Mapping the Two Faces of R&D: Productivity Growth in a Panel of OECD Industries." *Review of Economics and Statistics* 86 (4): 883–95.

Lucking, Brian, Nick Bloom, and John Van Reenen. 2017. "Have R&D Spillovers Changed?" CEP Discussion Paper 1548, Centre for Economic Performance, London.

Maloney, William F., and Felipe Valencia Caicedo. 2017. "Engineering Growth: Innovative Capacity and Development in the Americas." CESifo Working Paper 6339, Munich Society for the Promotion of Economic Research, Munich.

Mohnen, Pierre, and Bronwyn Hall. 2013. "Innovation and Productivity: An Update." *Eurasian Business Review* 3 (1): 47–65.

Schumpeter, Joseph A. 2008 (c1934). *The Theory of Economic Development: An Inquiry into Profits, Capital, Credit, Interest, and the Business Cycle.* Piscataway, NJ: Transaction Publishers.

Sutton, John. 2012. *Competing in Capabilities: The Globalization Process.* Oxford, UK: Oxford University Press.

Syverson, Chad. 2011. "What Determines Productivity?" *Journal of Economic Literature* 49 (2): 326–65.

World Bank. 2019a. "Impact Evaluation of EMPRETECNO Initiative." World Bank, Washington, DC.

World Bank. 2019b. "Public Expenditure Review of the National Innovation System in Argentina, 2019." World Bank, Washington, DC.

2 Innovation Performance

This chapter uses an "innovation function analysis" to benchmark Argentina's performance across a range of both innovation inputs, such as human capital, public and private research and development (R&D), managerial practices, and innovation outputs, such as patents and new businesses, products, and processes. Then it discusses the impact of these inputs and outputs on innovation performance.

INNOVATION INPUTS

Figure 2.1 describes the innovation function. This starts with innovation inputs and knowledge activities, which feed into innovation outputs and outcomes.

FIGURE 2.1

Innovation function: Innovation inputs and knowledge activities

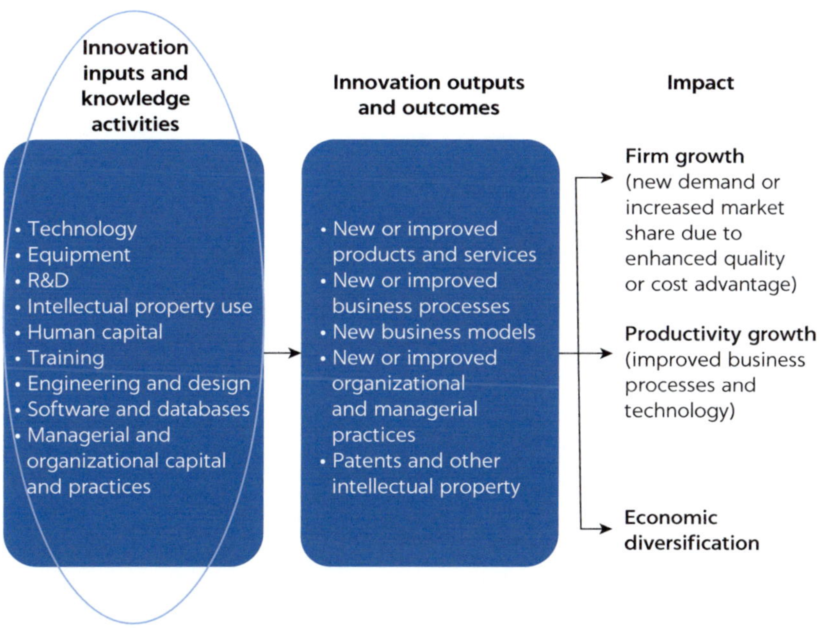

Source: Cirera and Maloney 2017.
Note: R&D = research and development.

In sum, these activities result in impacts on firm growth, productivity growth, and economic diversification.

Research and development

Research and development are critical inputs for innovation. However, similar to its regional peers, Argentina's gross expenditure on R&D (GERD) is low. Argentina invests 0.53 percent of its gross domestic product (GDP) in R&D—the second highest gross expenditure in Latin America after Brazil, which invests 1.2 percent of GDP. As shown in figure 2.2, between 2007 and 2015 Argentina increased total R&D expenditures by 78 percent (current purchasing power parity [PPP] US dollars) and its ratio of R&D to GDP by 15 percent (from 0.46 percent to 0.53 percent), similar to Chile (16 percent), Mexico (16 percent), and Brazil (18 percent). Despite this relative progress, Argentina's GERD is still much lower than the average for new high-income countries (1.3 percent) and way behind the average for Organisation for Economic Co-operation and Development (OECD) countries (2.4 percent) (figure 2.3). Such low expenditure on R&D weakens Argentina's ability to achieve high growth.

Recent estimates for the United States and Spain put returns to R&D at a striking 40–60 percent annually. Results are significant for low- and middle-income countries, too. R&D facilitates both advances at the technological frontier and catch-up by building the absorptive capacity of firms; most studies find it to be robustly related to innovation (Cirera and Maloney 2017). Analysis using World Bank Enterprise Survey data finds that, even when controlling more directly for causality, R&D significantly relates to product innovation (Cirera and Maloney 2017). Indeed, since the 1980s, high R&D intensity as well as a strong share of business spending in R&D have characterized high-growth low- and middle-income economies. If trends continue, China is poised to become the top R&D performer in the world by the end of the decade.[1]

Argentina performs especially poorly in private R&D spending. While Argentina's GERD is low but similar to that of its regional peers (figure 2.4), its business share of gross expenditure in R&D is the lowest among both its regional and its structural peers (17 percent compared to as high as 50 percent for Turkey). Although a higher share of businesses report spending on R&D in Argentina than in Malaysia and Turkey (figure 2.5), the share of private R&D

FIGURE 2.2

Spending on science and technology as a percentage of GDP in Argentina, 1992–2015

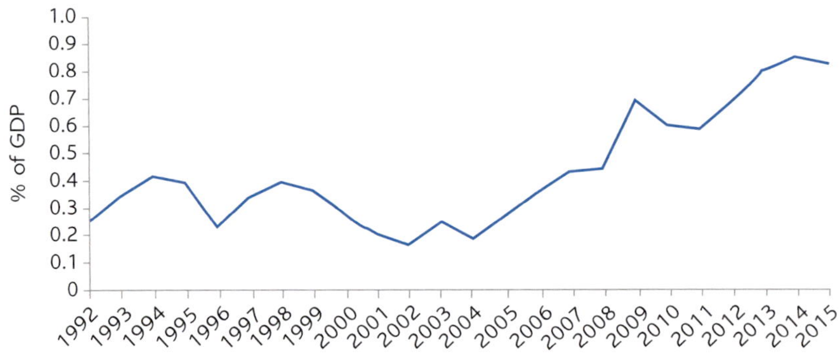

Source: World Bank 2019a.

FIGURE 2.3

Gross domestic spending on R&D in selected countries, 2007–17

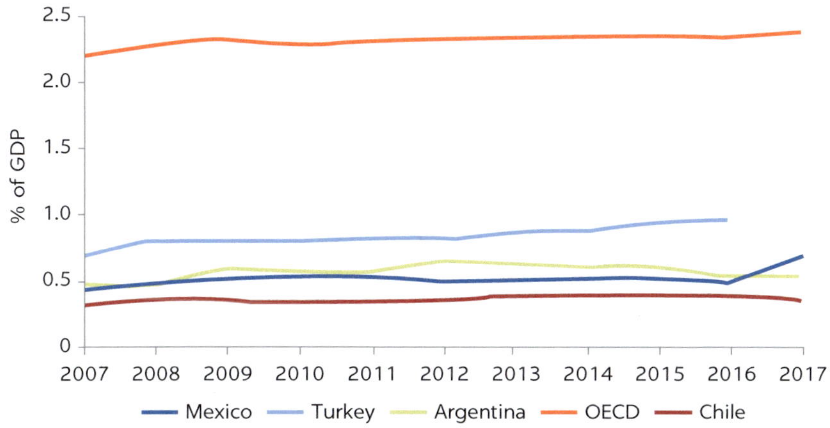

Source: OECD, Main Science and Technology Indicators Database: https://www.oecd.org/sti/msti.htm.
Note: OECD = Organisation for Economic Co-operation and Development; R&D = research and development.

FIGURE 2.4

Gross spending on R&D as a percentage of GDP in Argentina and selected countries, by source, 2017

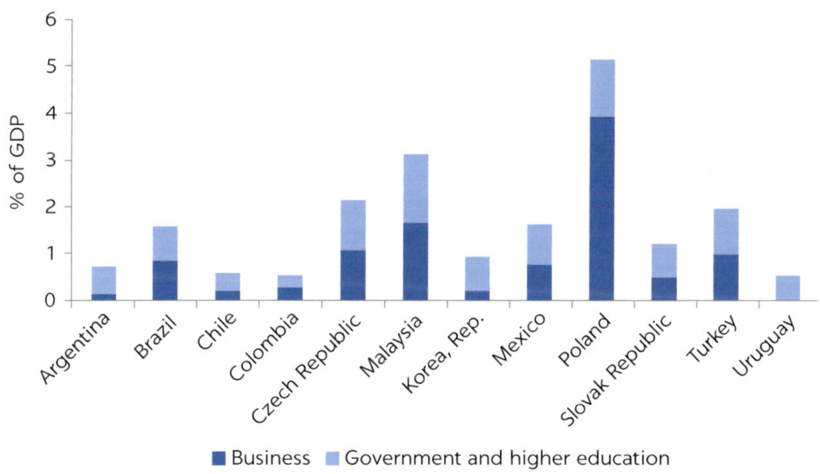

Source: World Bank 2017.
Note: R&D = research and development.

expenditures by value fell by 21 percent between 2007 and 2016 (Arza et al. 2020) (figure 2.6). Local entrepreneurs report low levels of technology adoption, and only one Argentine firm is found among the world's 1,000 largest publicly listed corporate R&D spenders (Jaruzelski, Chwalik, and Goehle 2018; WEF 2018). Private R&D expenditure accounts for only 0.09 percent of GDP, which is infinitesimal compared with the private R&D spending of world leaders such as China, whose private R&D investments represented 27 percent of the world's total in 2017, almost on par with US firms and up from a negligible 2 percent in 1996.

Figures 2.4 and 2.5 show gross spending on R&D as a percentage of GDP and the percentage of firms that invest in R&D activities, respectively, for Argentina and selected other countries.

FIGURE 2.5

Share of firms that invest in R&D in Argentina and selected countries

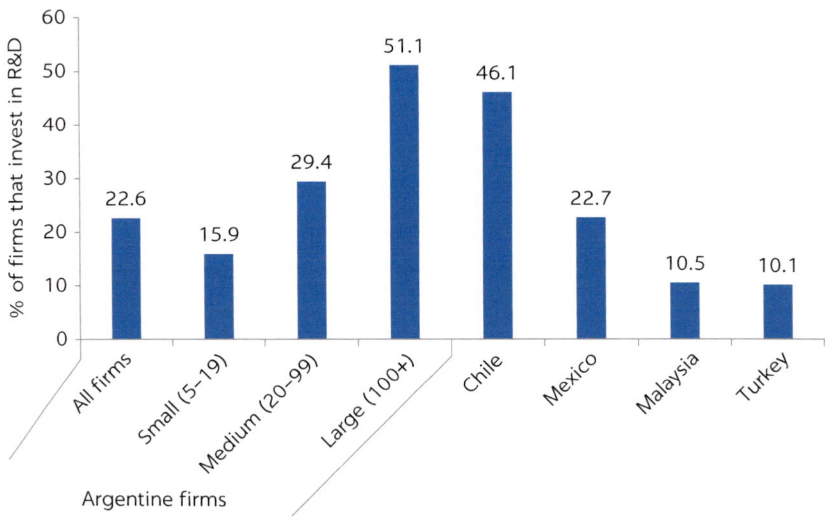

Source: World Bank 2017.
Note: Years available between 2012 and 2017. Firm sizes are differentiated by number of employees. R&D = research and development.

FIGURE 2.6

Share of R&D expenditures by firms to total R&D in Argentina and selected countries, 2007–16

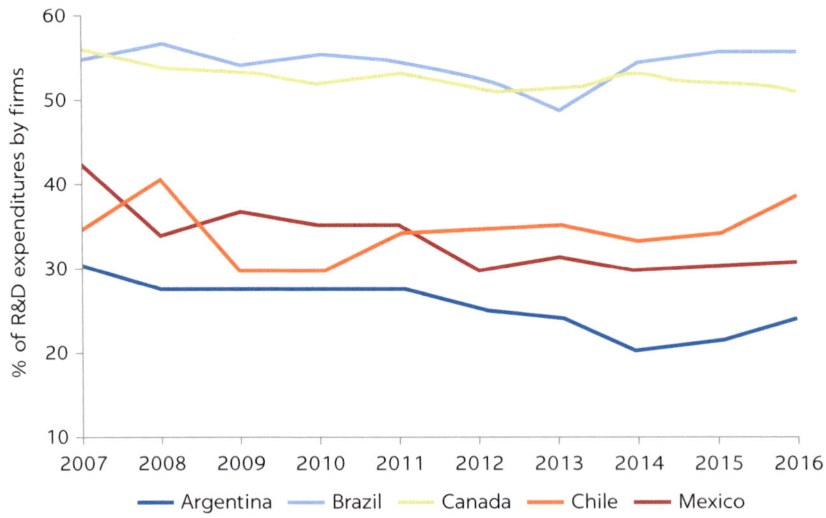

Source: Network for Science and Technology Indicators (RICYT) data.
Note: R&D = research and development.

Similarly, limited private sector participation in R&D is also manifested in the percentage of researchers employed by the private sector (figure 2.7). Even though Argentina produces more researchers per capita than its regional peers, a vast majority are employed by public agencies and only 13 percent of manufacturing firms have an R&D department. In Argentina, businesses employ as little as 9 percent of all researchers, a smaller share than across all of

FIGURE 2.7

Share of researchers employed by the private sector in Argentina and selected countries, 2017

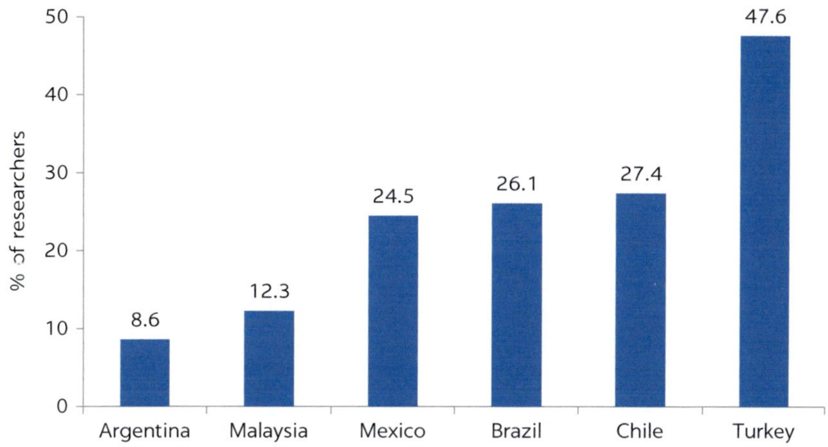

Source: World Bank 2017.

its comparators. Turkey, for example, produces slightly more researchers per capita than Argentina, but as much as 48 percent are employed by the private sector (figure 2.7).

Technology absorption and equipment

In addition to limited investments in R&D, other important channels of technology transfer are also underused. Businesses' ability to upgrade is further hindered by the limited use of foreign technology licenses and equipment. Licensing of technology and purchases of equipment and training are some of the main channels for knowledge absorption in low- and middle-income countries. For example, more than 75 percent of Turkish firms and 45 percent of Asian firms indicate that they acquire knowledge mostly through the purchase of machinery and equipment, as opposed to other possible sources of knowledge (World Bank 2005). In Argentina, however, only 44 percent of firms[2] report having invested in fixed assets (which include land and buildings in addition to equipment and machinery) (World Bank 2017). Argentina's total spending on computer software is 0.2 percent of GDP, similar to that of its regional peers but behind Malaysia and Turkey, which spend up to 0.5 percent of GDP on computer software. Similarly, as few as 7.5 percent of firms in Argentina report using technology licensed from foreign companies, compared with 20 percent in Turkey (figure 2.8).

Human capital and research

Despite weaknesses in R&D investments and technology transfer, Argentina has assets—researchers and excellent research institutes—that support innovation. Between 2004 and 2016, Argentina expanded its research base by 36 percent (to 3.006 researchers per 1,000 employees), representing the highest regional increase and placing it ahead of comparators such as Chile and Mexico (between 0.8 and 1.1). Argentina now has the highest number of researchers per capita in

FIGURE 2.8

Share of firms using foreign technology licenses in Argentina and selected countries, 2017

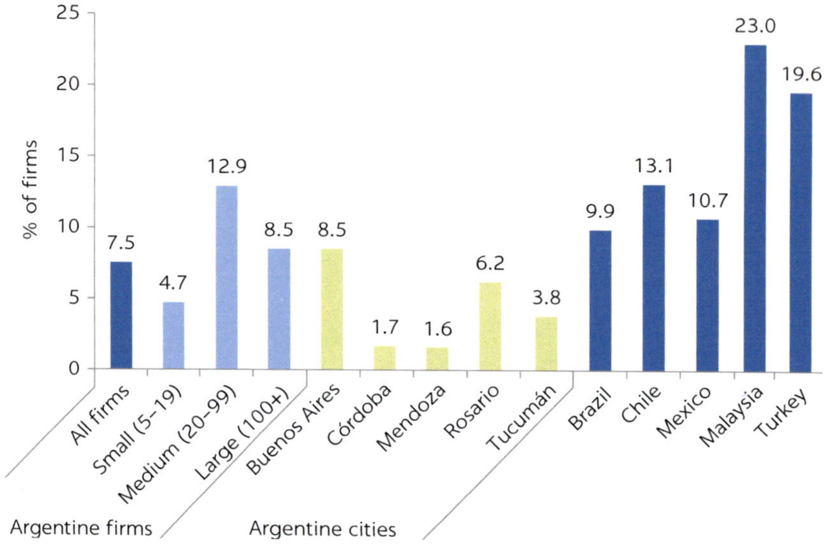

Source: World Bank 2017.
Note: Firm sizes are differentiated by number of employees.

FIGURE 2.9

Researchers per 1,000 employed in Argentina and selected countries, 2007–17

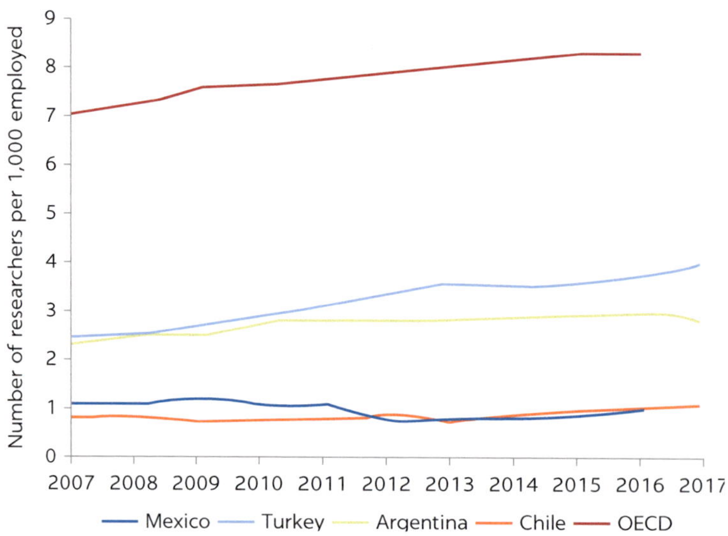

Source: OECD, Main Science and Technology Indicators Database: https://www.oecd.org/sti/msti.htm.
Note: OECD = Organisation for Economic Co-operation and Development.

Latin America and ranks especially well in terms of the excellence of its research centers, at 27th in the world in 2019—ahead of all of its regional and most of its structural peers (figures 2.9 and 2.10). Box 2.1 provides further details on two of Argentina's research organizations. The contribution of health and education to worker productivity in Argentina, at 0.61 as measured by the human capital index,[3] is also slightly above the Latin American and Caribbean average of 0.56. In terms of academic links with the global research community, Argentina also ranks among the highest in the region, with international co-invention representing

FIGURE 2.10

Excellence of research organizations in Argentina and selected countries, 2007–17

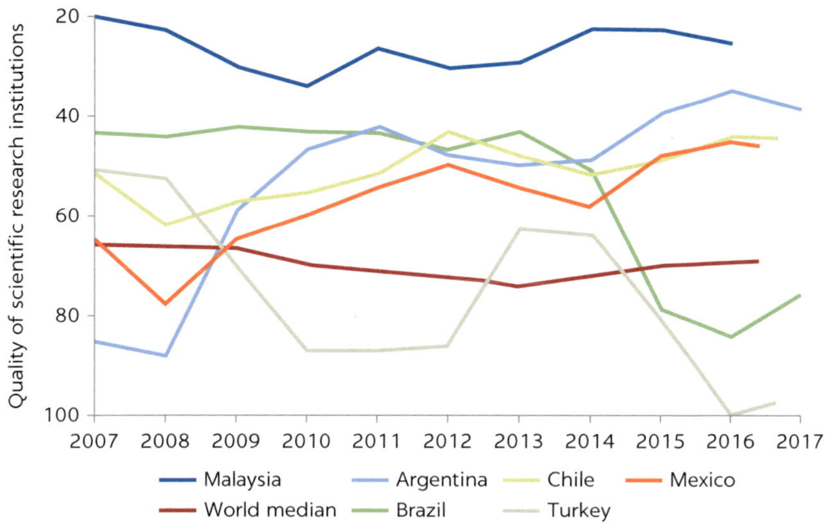

Source: WEF 2018.
Note: 1 = the best ranking.

BOX 2.1

Public research institutions in Argentina

- *The National Science and Technical Research Council (CONICET)* is the main science and technology organization in Argentina, with more than 10,000 full-time researchers and agreements with the main universities and other science and technology organizations across the country. CONICET was established in 1958 by Nobel Prize winner Bernardo Houssay as an enclave of academic excellence. CONICET submits the largest number of annual patent applications to the National Institute of Industrial Property of Argentina. In 2017, CONICET requested 75 patents worldwide, out of which 33 were new inventions. These patents ranged from industrial design to software patents.
- *Estación Experimental (EEAOC)* in Tucumán was founded in 1909 by the visionary leader Alejandro Guzmán. Funded largely by the association of sugarcane producers, EEAOC boosted the Argentine economy with the large-scale introduction of a genetic variety of soya in the 1970s and 1980. Before that, soya had been cultivated for a long time, but only on a limited basis. EEAOC introduced and has continuously improved three commercial export crops—sugarcane, lemons (and other citrus), and soya. The internal rate of return for these three products is high. Over the period 1960–2009, for each peso invested in the research, development, and extension of those crops, the internal rate of return was 25.33 percent for sugarcane, 20.54 percent for soya, and 29.35 percent for lemons. These numbers measure only the effects in Tucumán; they do not capture externalities beyond the province.

41.79 percent of total Patent Co-operation Treaty patents and international co-authorship representing 88 percent of total scientific articles (OECD 2014).

However, the links between public research and private sector are limited. In Argentina, despite noteworthy progress since 2007, the impact of innovation is still affected by the limited degree to which public research organizations and businesses collaborate effectively. While there are strong networks of research institutions and some highly respected public universities, productivity-enhancing partnerships with the private sector have historically been few and far between. According to the 2019 Global Innovation Index (GII),[4] Argentina scores the lowest among its structural and regional peers in innovation links (Cornell University, INSEAD, and WIPO 2018).[5] It is one of the worst performers in the world, ranking 108th among the 128 countries, as measured by the 2019 GII.

According to a survey conducted by the World Economic Forum among countries' executives, most Argentine businesses report little collaboration with universities on R&D and complain about the absence of deep clusters that enhance and promote productive innovation (WEF 2018). The absence of links is not only a weakness in the innovation function, but also a lost opportunity for Argentina, which needs to take advantage of its strengths, including those in research. The larger literature on national innovation systems extensively discusses the importance and dynamic nature of the links among government institutions, the private sector, and universities. For example, Bosch, Lederman, and Maloney (2005) suggest that the security of intellectual property rights, the quality of research institutions, and the degree of collaboration with the private sector explain half of the difference in the elasticity of knowledge creation between advanced and follower countries. Public-private partnerships have been at center stage in countries such as the Republic of Korea, Japan, and Singapore. In Argentina, while recent policy measures have sought to realign incentives between public research and the productive sector, much more remains to be done to increase the number of public-private partnerships that can contribute to the innovation function in Argentina (figure 2.11). Appendix B presents two case studies: CONICET and EEAOC and Chapter 4 discusses a recent initiative with successful results (FONARSEC).

Despite strengths in research and research institutions, gaps remain in human capital inputs, especially in science, technology, engineering, and mathematics (STEM) and entrepreneurship. In education, Argentina performs relatively better at the two ends of the spectrum—primary education and research. The share of population ages 25–34 with less than a secondary school education was 32 percent in 2014, lower than in Brazil (36 percent), Turkey (45 percent), and Mexico (53 percent); however, in terms of the ratio of the total number of bachelor's, master's, and PhD degrees to total population, Argentina still lags Chile and Brazil. In particular, Argentina performs poorly in the number of STEM graduates, an important indicator of the ability

FIGURE 2.11

Innovation links in Argentina and selected countries, 2018

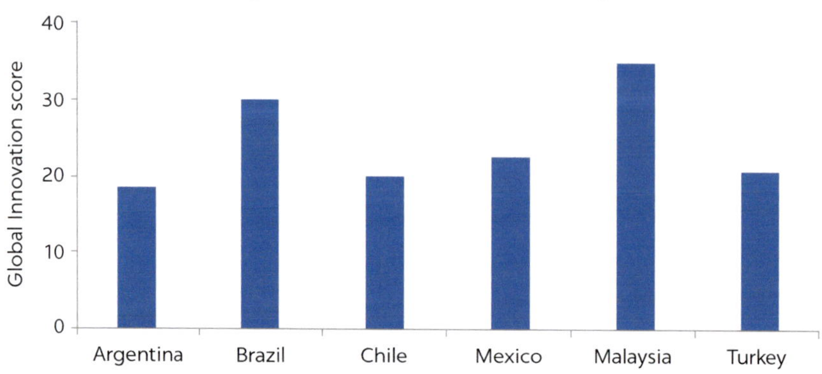

Source: Cornell University, INSEAD, and WIPO 2018.

of firms to innovate. While slightly ahead of Brazil, Argentina is below its structural peers in the percentage of graduates in these disciplines and is second-lowest among OECD countries (figures 2.12 and 2.13).

Moreover, early entrepreneurship has been declining in Argentina. Defined as the percentage of the population ages 18–64 who are either nascent entrepreneurs or owner-managers of a new business, early entrepreneurship fell from 20 percent in 2011 to 6 percent in 2017; in 2017 it was lower than in its regional and structural peers (in Mexico and Turkey, with the next lowest rates, it was about 15 percent). Considering Argentina's recent demographics, today about 1.2 million individuals are engaging in some form of early-stage entrepreneurial activity; given the rates in 2011, as many as 4 million explored entrepreneurship only a few years back—suggesting a huge untapped potential and low firm survival rates and pointing to a significant number of would-be entrepreneurs who are constrained by factors ranging from a challenging macro context to limited

FIGURE 2.12

Share of tertiary graduates in STEM fields in Argentina and selected countries, average 2012–17

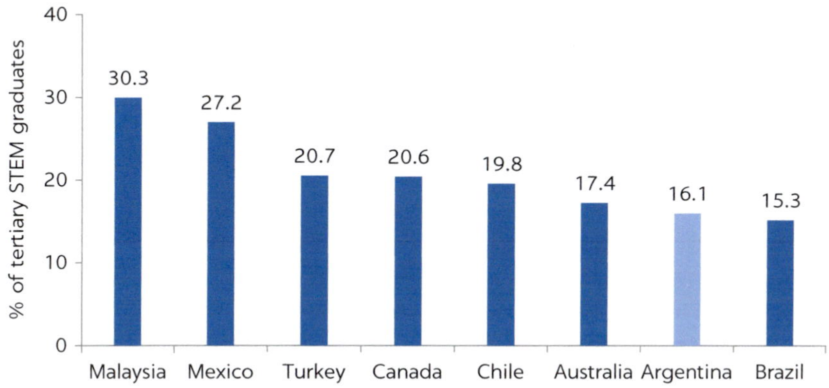

Source: UNESCO data.
Note: Years available between 2012 and 2017 differ across countries. STEM = science, technology, engineering, and mathematics.

FIGURE 2.13

Share of tertiary graduates in STEM fields in Argentina and the OECD

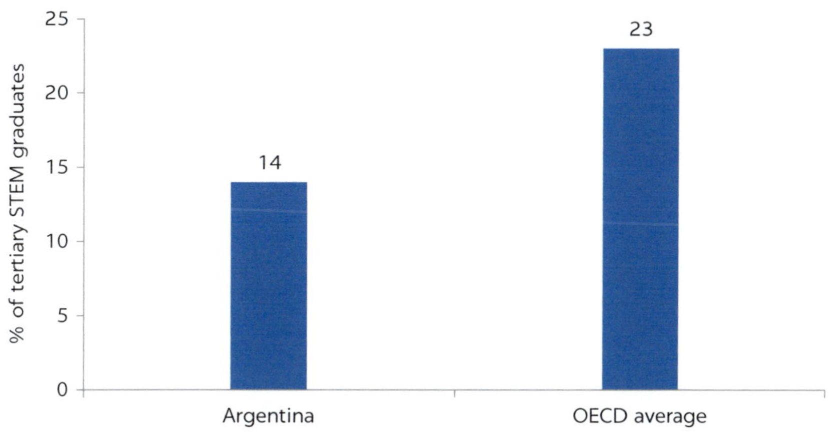

Source: UNESCO data.
Note: OECD = Organisation for Economic Co-operation and Development; STEM = science, technology, engineering, and mathematics.

FIGURE 2.14
Management score in Argentina and selected countries, 2019

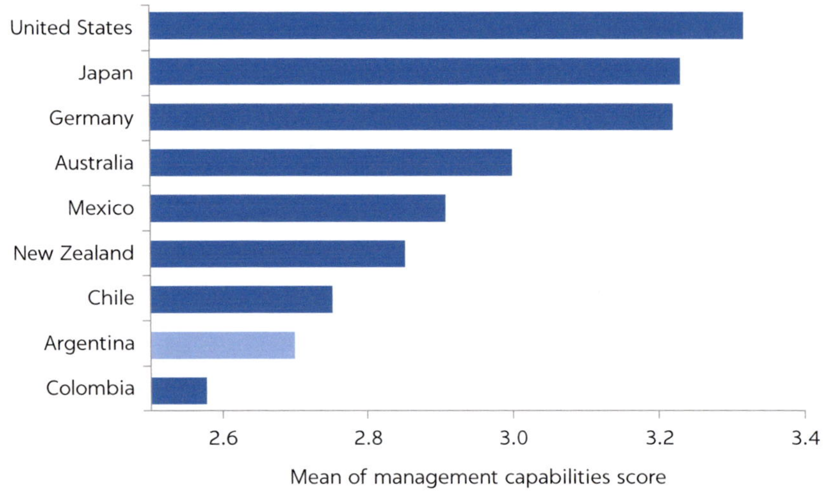

Source: World Management Index; Castro et al., 2021.

access to finance and lack of managerial capabilities. These constraints translate into low density of new businesses.

The declining rate of early entrepreneurship is a concern for a country that needs to improve its economic growth sustainably and create jobs. Most start-ups are more effective in exploiting new technologies and introducing radical innovations (Almeida and Kogut 1997; Baumol 2002; Zucker, Darby, and Peng 1998). Moreover, global evidence suggests that the small proportion of start-ups that grow to become transformational entrepreneurs—on average 4 percent—creates a disproportionate number of new jobs. For example, out of 100 jobs created over a five-year period, between 22 (the Netherlands) and 53 (France) newly created jobs came from this group (OECD 2016). Moreover, the rapid scale-up of a small number of very successful start-ups was one of the main drivers of aggregate employment growth.

Finally, in Argentina, the quality of management is among the worst in the region. Management capabilities, as measured by the World Management Survey, are poor, independent of the sector (figure 2.14). Low performance hinders the ability of firms to grow, create employment, export, and innovate. Furthermore, managers are unaware of these failures. As indicated by comparing self-scores to management practice test scores, managers in Argentina are prone to overestimating their capabilities. The existence of information asymmetries suggests that public policy has a role to play in affecting behavior and forming management capability.

INNOVATION OUTPUTS

Argentina lags both its regional and its structural peers when it comes to firm-level innovation and knowledge and technology outputs such as new businesses and patents (figure 2.15). According to the 2019 GII, Argentina's composite score for innovation outputs, which include knowledge, technology, and creative outputs such as patents, ISO 9001 certificates, and share of high-tech exports, among others, lags that of all regional and structural comparators.

FIGURE 2.15

Innovation function: Innovation outputs and outcomes

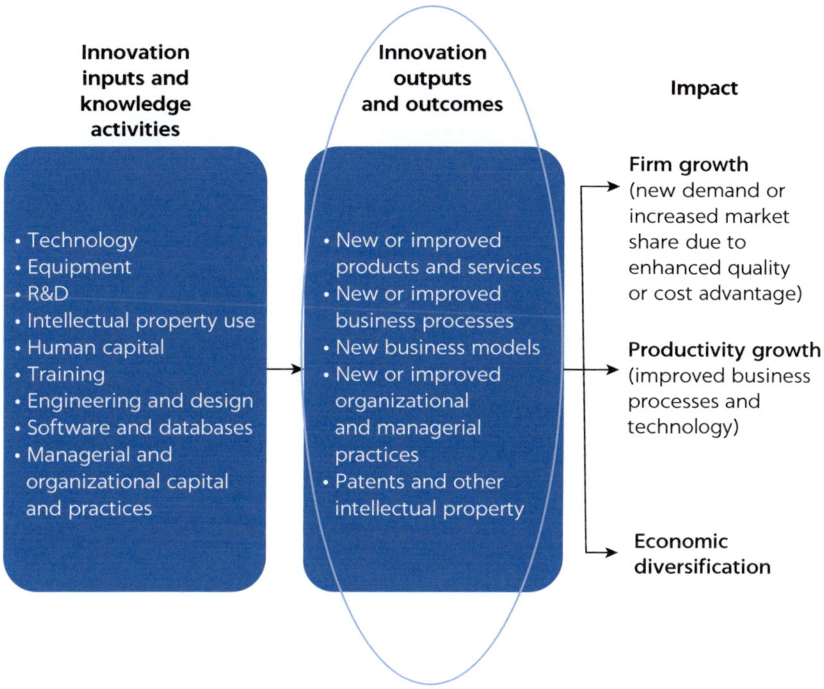

Source: Cirera and Maloney 2017.
Note: R&D = research and development.

FIGURE 2.16

Resident patent applications in Argentina and selected countries, 2017

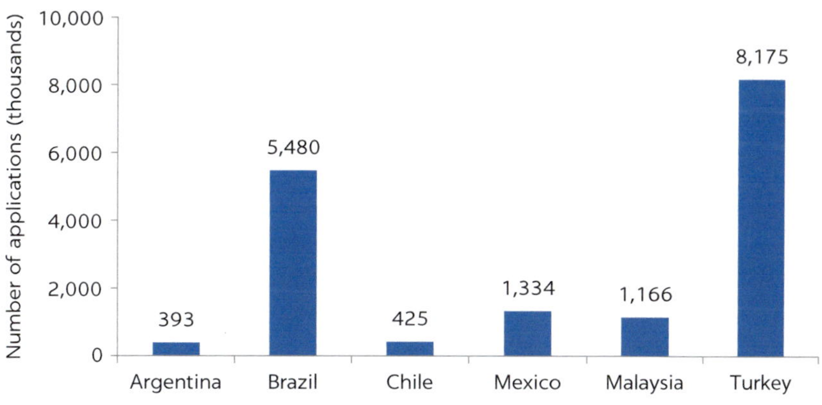

Source: World Intellectual Property Organization data.

Argentina ranks 75th in the world, behind even lower-income economies such as Jamaica and Kenya. Its rate of patent applications per capita is the lowest among all peers—at less than 10 percent of the patent applications filed in Turkey (figure 2.16). As a result, the annual number of patents granted as a proportion of expenditure in R&D is especially low. Moreover, international trademark applications per person are lower in Argentina than in Chile or Costa Rica (World Bank 2019c) and the share of high-tech exports in total exports is only 2 percent. Regarding the number of ISO 9001 certificates issued or citable documents, Argentina is significantly ahead of Brazil and Turkey when adjusted for the size of these economies. However, regarding the density and growth of new businesses, measured as a share of GDP per worker (in PPP dollars, a measure of labor productivity), Argentina is significantly behind all comparator economies. Other types of firm-level innovation are limited, too. Among (formal) manufacturing firms, more than 50 percent did not introduce a new product or service, and more than 60 percent did not introduce a process innovation in 2017 (World Bank 2017).

Overall, weaknesses and gaps across innovation inputs and outputs paint a checkered scorecard for Argentina. As of 2019, Argentina ranked 73th in the GII, significantly below Chile (51), Mexico (56), Turkey (49), Brazil (66), and Malaysia (35). This weakness is due in part to gaps across the innovation function and the inability to transform some of Argentina's strong capabilities in science and technology into private sector and growth outcomes; however, three sets of factors also underpin innovation's limited contribution: macro complementarities, firm-level capabilities, and policy weaknesses. In Argentina, these factors are complicated by the regional economic heterogeneity and varying market failures in different provinces, which are discussed further in appendix A.

INNOVATION IMPACTS

Innovation has not yet made significant contributions to aggregate productivity growth in Argentina. Argentina lags behind all of its structural and regional peers across three levels of impact expected from a successful innovation function: firm growth, productivity growth, and economic diversification (figure 2.17).

Firm growth and new business creation are low. Argentina's economy is mired in slow private sector growth and a lack of dynamism from new entrants. According to World Bank Enterprise Surveys for 2010 and 2017, labor

FIGURE 2.17

Innovation function: Impact

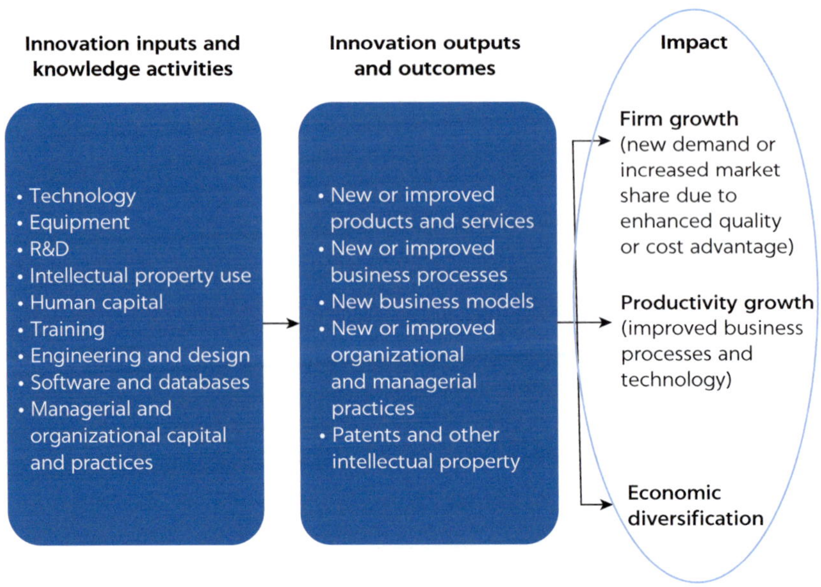

Source: Cirera and Maloney 2017.
Note: R&D = research and development.

productivity at the firm level fell an average of close to 6 percent in those years. The majority of Argentine enterprises consist of small companies with low and sluggish productivity, characterized by a "stunted growth" syndrome, where mature businesses do not grow significantly larger than new entrants (figure 2.18). Few firms in Argentina manage to grow sustainably; after five years, most existing micro, small, and medium enterprises remain the same size (while a mature firm in the United States after the same period of time is nine times the size of a start-up). As a result, the proportion of fast-growing firms—those that generate most new private employment—is small. Similarly, despite significant entrepreneurship potential, new business density (new business registrations per 1,000 people ages 15–65) has been historically low, declining slightly since 2008. According to the latest data available (2014), there was only 0.43 new business for every 1,000 people, as opposed to 0.86, 1.00, and 3.20 for Brazil, Turkey, and OECD members, respectively (World Bank 2019c) (figure 2.19).

In the absence of firm growth and private sector dynamism, productivity-led growth has been limited. Since 1960, the contribution of total factor productivity (TFP) has been erratic, decreasing in three of the last six decades for an average of zero growth, compared with a 0.6 percent average annual growth rate in OECD countries and new high-income countries. A recent diagnosis of growth in Argentina shows that since 2012 TFP has made a negative contribution to growth (World Bank 2019a). Furthermore, changes in TFP have contributed to the volatility of growth. The contribution of capital has been decreasing, with the ratio of capital to GDP falling, on average, by 15 percent since the 1980s. The combination of stagnant TFP and declining capital intensity ratio has led to relatively low growth of labor productivity (figure 2.20).

Lagging TFP contributes to poor economic complexity and low export sophistication. Unsophisticated, unprocessed products—primarily in the agriculture sector—still dominate Argentina's export basket. Vegetables and foodstuffs are the two largest categories of exports, representing more than 50 percent of Argentina's export basket (figure 2.21). While the dominance of agriculture

FIGURE 2.18

Distribution of companies and employment in Argentina, by firm size, 2017

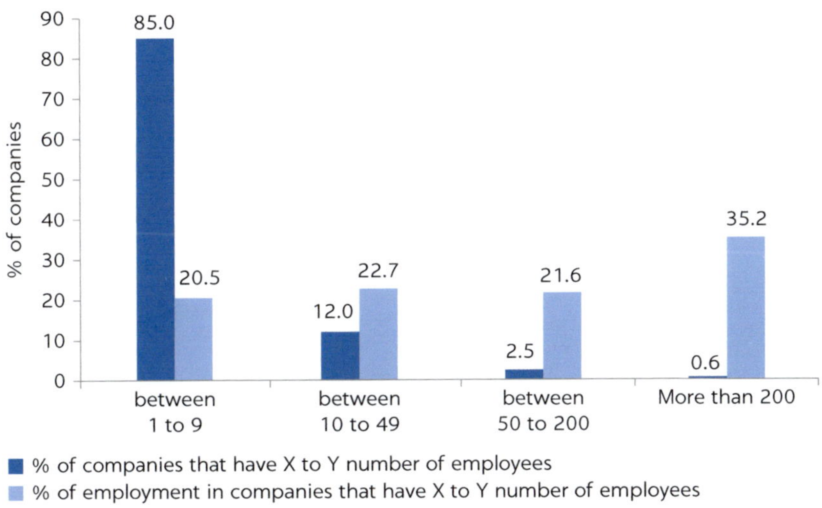

Source: GPS Empresas, Ministry of Production, Argentina.

FIGURE 2.19

Density of new business creation in Argentina and selected countries, 2007–16

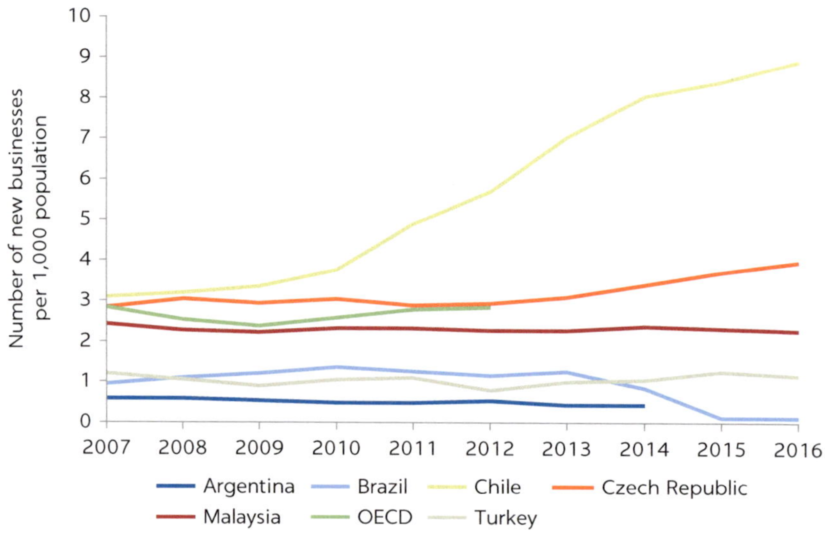

Source: World Bank data.

FIGURE 2.20

Changes in total factor productivity in Argentina and selected countries, 2010–14

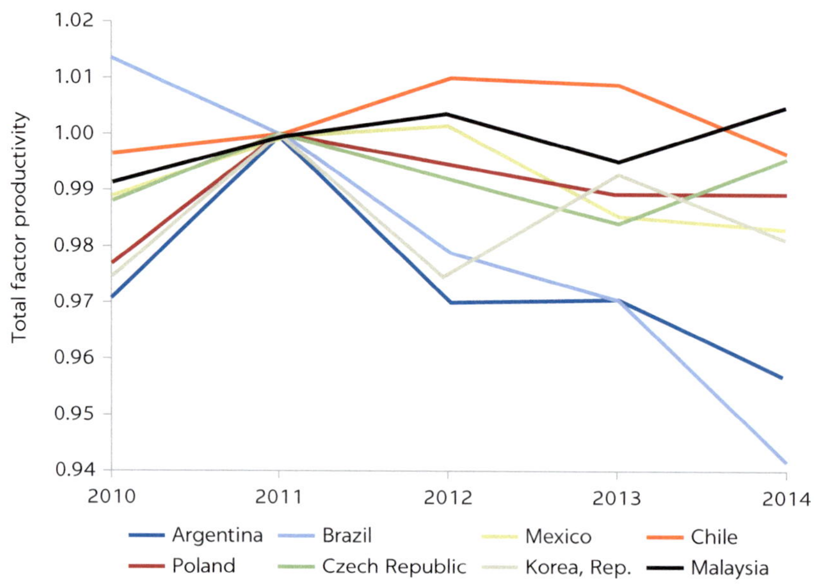

Source: World Bank 2019a.

has persisted and even increased since 1995, the global competitiveness of Argentine exports, including in agriculture, has decreased. Argentina's global market share in agriculture has declined from 3.4 percent in 2008 to 2.7 percent in 2015, contributing to an overall decrease in Argentina's global share of exports.[6] Overall, Argentina had the lowest export growth between 2010 and 2017 among

FIGURE 2.21

Exports of Argentina, 2017

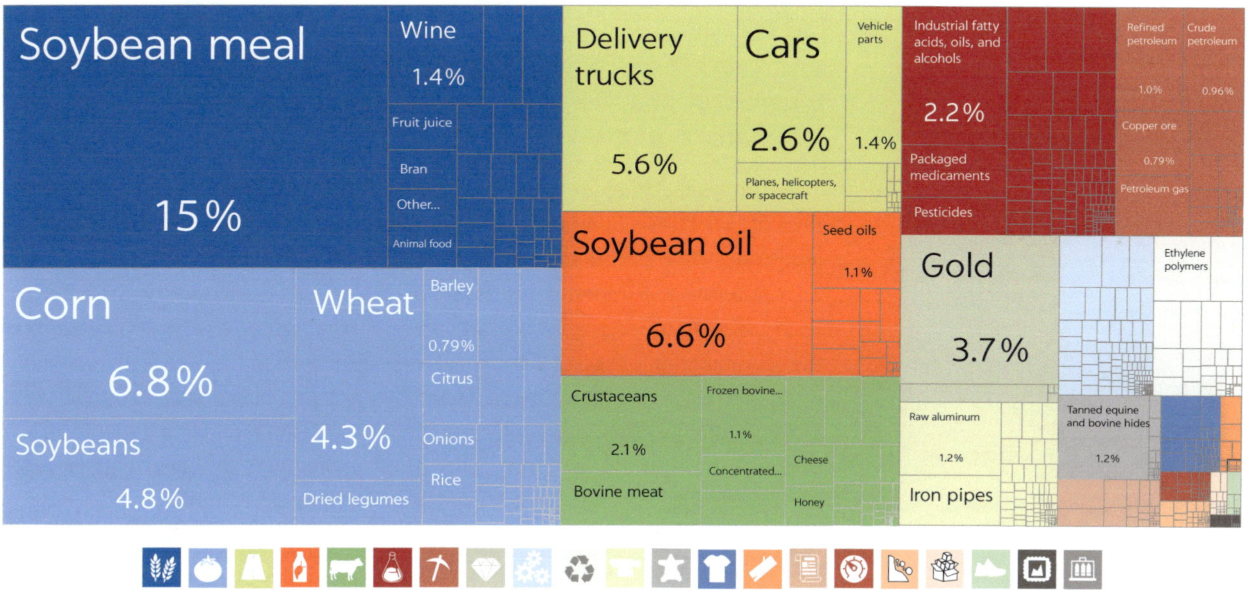

Source: Harvard Observatory of Economic Complexity (2017 data).

FIGURE 2.22

Economic complexity index score for Argentina and selected countries, 2007–17

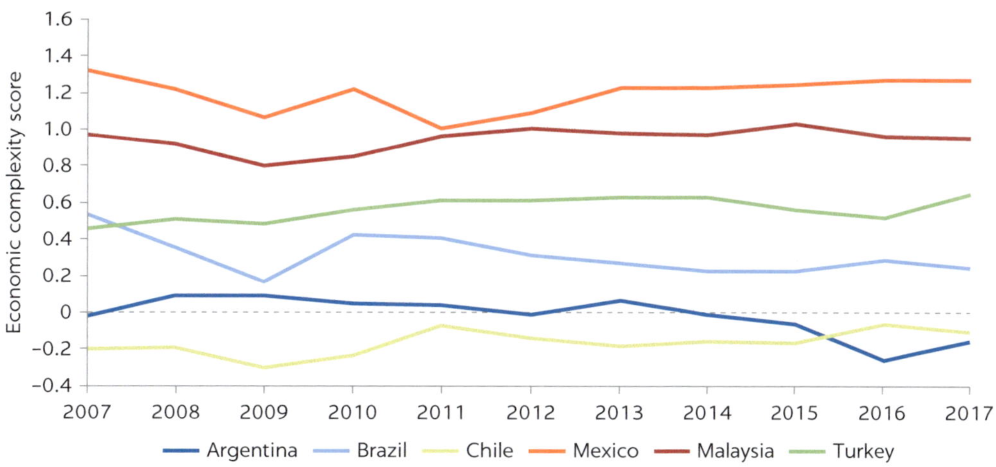

Source: Atlas of Economic Complexity, Center for International Development at Harvard University.

comparator countries, with a negative average annual growth rate of 1.3 percent (World Bank 2019b). According toHarvard University's Atlas of Economic Complexity,[7] in 2017, Argentina ranked 72th out of 133 countries, behind regional peers like Chile (69), Brazil (48), and Mexico (20), as well as structural peers like Malaysia (28) and Turkey (38); Argentina also has experienced a relative decline in economic complexity since the mid-1990s, when it ranked ahead of both Chile and Turkey (figure 2.22).

FACTORS EXPLAINING INNOVATION'S LIMITED CONTRIBUTIONS TO PRODUCTIVITY AND GROWTH OUTCOMES

Imbalances and distortions in the macro and micro foundations of growth

The structural challenges in the macro and micro foundations weaken the incentives of firms to accumulate innovation capabilities. In a context of high country risk (figure 2.23), regular current account and fiscal crises, high inflation, and restrictions in the trade regime as well as distortions to competition, businesses find it difficult to receive, absorb, and act on market signals that would incentivize the accumulation of knowledge. Moreover, distortions in the competitive dynamics of markets create allocative inefficiencies, possibly redirecting resources away from productive firms, while issues of openness and limited global integration further hurt the innovation function by limiting channels of technology transfer through foreign direct investment and access to foreign technology.

Argentina's limited financial markets also hamper their ability to finance technology, innovation, and entrepreneurship in general. Accessing finance for innovation has higher thresholds than accessing other types of financing, due to the inherent information asymmetries. The firm seeking to innovate often has a more intimate knowledge of the innovation and more capacity to develop it than the external financing agent, which is likely to be skeptical of the innovation's returns. Overall, global experience stresses credit constraints (Aghion, Howitt, and Prantl 2012; Bond, Kutsenko, and Lozitskaya 2010; Hall, Mairesse, and Mohnen 2009; and Mulkay, Hall, and Mairesse 2000) and the depressing impact of uncertainty (Bloom 2007) as reasons for underinvestment in innovation. At 14 percent, Argentina's credit to the private sector remains especially low even in comparison to the rest of Latin America and the Caribbean (44 percent average), while interest rates historically average above 30 percent (climbing as high as 73 percent as of 2019) (figures 2.24 and 2.25). Consequently, financing for innovation and entrepreneurship financing is hit especially hard in Argentina.

Indeed, according to the Global Entrepreneurship Monitor, the availability of financing for entrepreneurs is lower in Argentina than in any of its regional and

FIGURE 2.23

Real effective exchange rate in Argentina and selected countries in Latin America, 2007–18

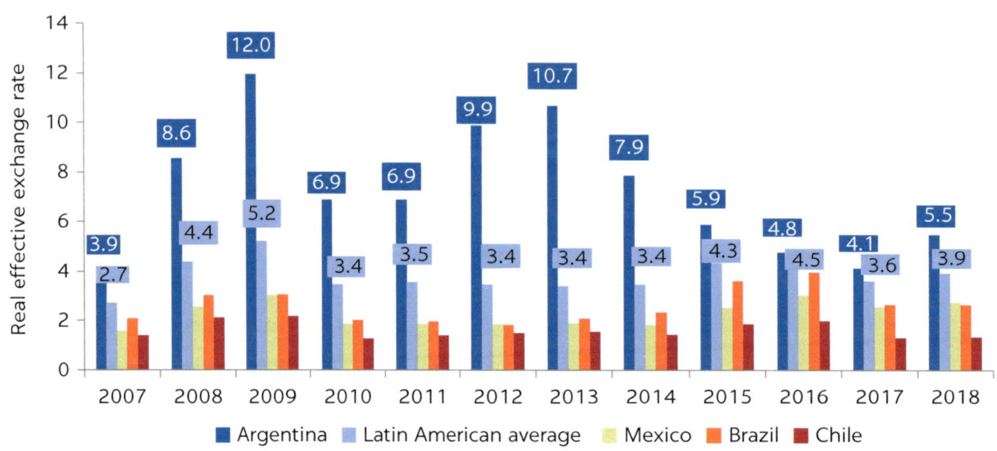

Source: Eurostat 2019.

FIGURE 2.24
Interest rates in Argentina, by firm size, 2018–19

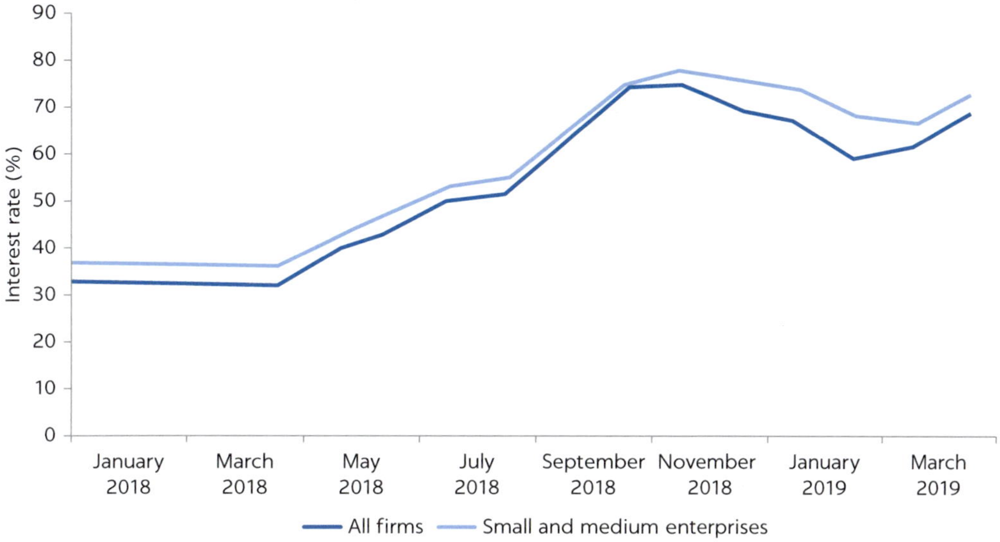

Source: Central Bank of Argentina.

FIGURE 2.25
Credit to private sector in Argentina and selected countries and regions, 2018

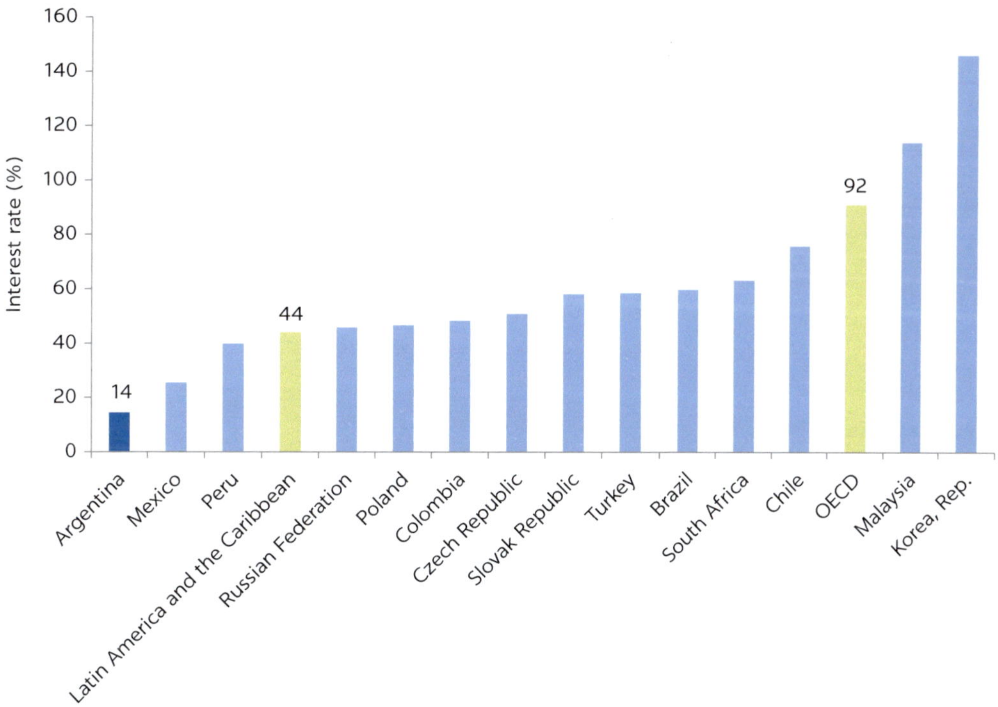

Source: Haver Analytics, International Financial Statistics 4Q 2018 data.
Note: OECD = Organisation for Economic Co-operation and Development.

structural peers, receiving a score of less than 2 out of 9 (figure 2.26). In terms of venture capital funding, rough estimates of US$100 million to US$200 million in funding commitments or venture capital funds raised in 2017–18 show a nascent but growing venture capital investment scene.[8] According to TechCrunch, more than 30 funding transactions worth US$3 million or more occurred in 2017.

FIGURE 2.26

Financing for entrepreneurs in Argentina and selected countries

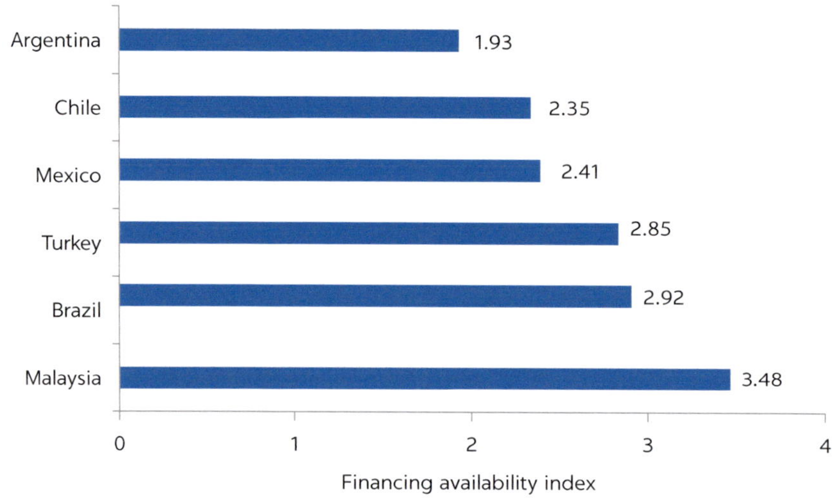

Source: Global Entrepreneurship Monitor, based on national expert surveys on financing for entrepreneurs: the availability of financial resources—equity and debt—for small and medium enterprises.
Note: 1 = very inadequate insufficient status; 9 = very adequate sufficient status.

FIGURE 2.27

Ratio of venture capital and private spending on R&D to GDP in Argentina and the OECD

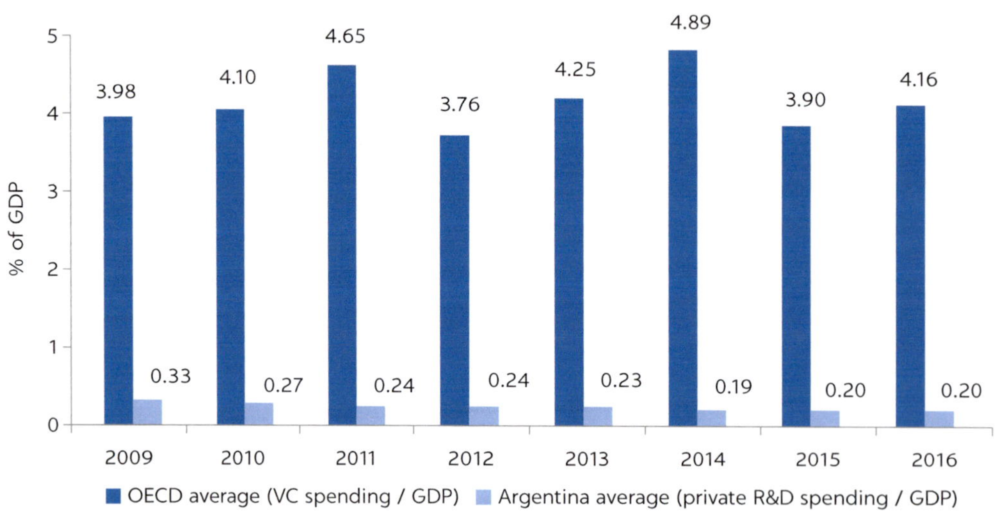

Source: Global Entrepreneurship Monitor, based on national expert surveys on financing for entrepreneurs: the availability of financial resources—equity and debt—for small and medium enterprises.
Note: OECD = Organisation for Economic Co-operation and Development; R&D = research and development; VC = venture capital.

Taking the high end of the estimate, total venture capital funding amounts to 0.03 percent of Argentina's US$637 billion 2017 GDP (figure 2.27). By contrast, according to OECD figures, the average OECD country spent 4.16 percent of GDP on venture capital in 2016.

Limited absorptive capacity of firms

In addition to the depressing effects of macro imbalances and market distortions, limited firm capabilities also explain the subpar contribution of innovation to economic growth. A recent study by Arza et al. (2020), using the National Survey of Employment Dynamics and Innovation (ENDEI), a micro innovation database, investigates the heterogeneity in returns to private R&D between sectors and regions in Argentina. Among others, they study the impact of managerial qualities on the effect of contextual factors that help or hurt returns to R&D. The study suggests that innovation capacity—for example, due to the quality of managerial practices—is likely to explain a portion of the observed heterogeneity in the returns to innovation, by means of taking better advantage of, or managing differently, context-based complementary factors. For example, it finds that, while context-based complementary factors such as policy uncertainty and competition affect returns to innovation in Argentina, as expected, the impact of improved market competition is higher when mediated by the attitudes of proactive firms. It also shows that returns to innovation through STI policy and intrasectoral spillovers are higher and positive (and significant only in the case of STI) if firms have innovative capacity that can economically appropriate the rewards of innovation in a specific context.

Argentina's experience here is in line with recent literature on the relationship between managerial practices and firm growth. These studies focus on the relationship between managerial practices and innovation outcomes, by studying four dimensions of management identified by industry experts: (a) *operations* in terms of the introduction of lean manufacturing and improvements, (b) *monitoring* for constant improvements, (c) use of appropriate *targets* and acting when problems arise, and (d) use of *incentives* to attract and retain talent and analyze their impact on firms' performance. They find that the quality of management practices is correlated not only with better innovation outcomes, but also with important innovation inputs such as R&D intensity. Maloney and Sarrias (2017) suggest that some of the heterogenous "innovative capacity" in transforming knowledge investments into productivity gains is related to the quality of managerial practices (figure 2.28, panel a).

FIGURE 2.28

Relationship between better management and the impact of R&D on innovation in Argentina and selected countries

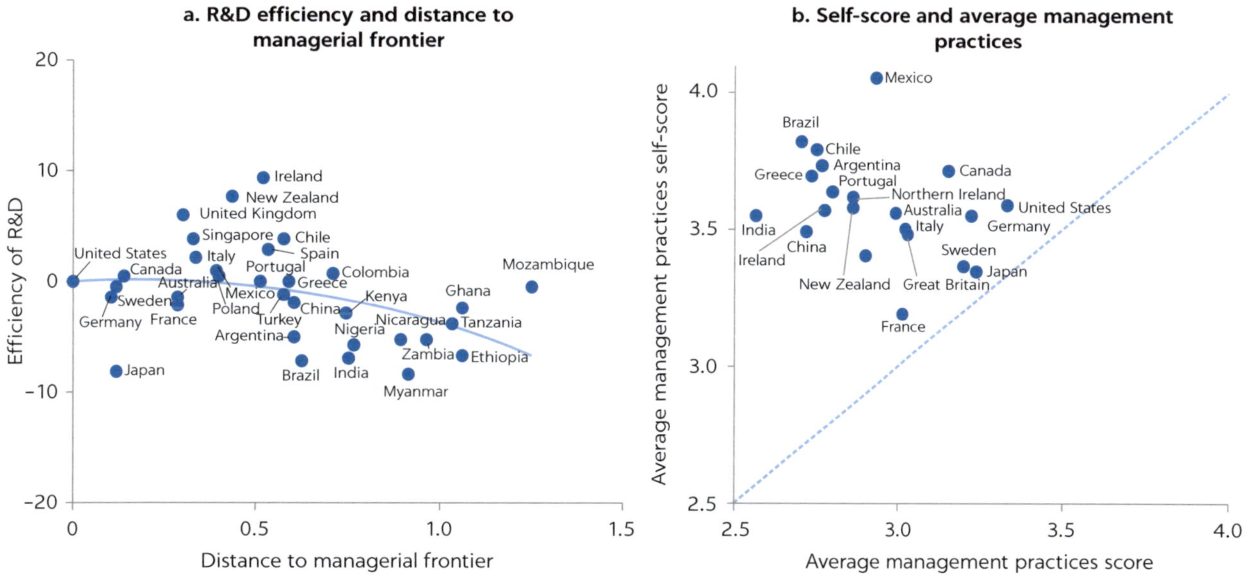

Source: Cirera and Maloney 2017, based on elaboration from Global Innovation Index 2015 and World Management Survey 2015.
Note: R&D = research and development.

Chapter 3 builds on the innovation function analysis presented in this chapter by reporting the findings of a "lite" public expenditure review of Argentina's policy response to the challenge of strengthening innovation.

NOTES

1. Despite a slowdown in growth compared with 2001–08, China's R&D expenditure doubled over 2008–12, and its R&D intensity is now on par with that of the European Union.
2. Close to 60 percent of these firms have significant foreign ownership and access to foreign networks and capital.
3. The human capital index (scale 0–1) calculates the contributions of health and education to worker productivity.
4. The GII measures 80 detailed, innovation-linked metrics from 129 economies and is one of the leading references for assessing an economy's innovation performance. In addition to rankings, each year a report is issued that focuses on a central theme pertinent to innovation-related issues for that year. The GII is a joint publication of Cornell University College of Business, INSEAD, and the World Intellectual Property Organization (WIPO). The overall ranking measures seven subindicators, broken into innovation inputs and innovation outputs. Innovation inputs include institutions, human capital and research, infrastructure, market sophistication, and business sophistication. Innovation outputs include knowledge and technology outputs and creative outputs. Each subindicator measures more granular variables, all of which aggregate up to the overall GII ranking. For more information, see https://www.globalinnovationindex.org/home.
5. Innovation links are broadly defined as research-oriented commercial projects that are shared between universities and businesses. The score draws on both qualitative and quantitative data regarding business-university collaboration on R&D, the prevalence of well-developed and deep clusters, the level of gross R&D expenditure financed abroad, and the number of deals on joint ventures and strategic alliances.
6. World Bank, World Integrated Trade Solutions (WITS) database, https://wits.worldbank.org.
7. See http://www.atlas.cid.harvard.edu.
8. See, for example, https://techcrunch.com/2018/07/27/in-argentina-venture-capital-surges-even-as-the-broader-economy-stutters/ and https://www.nathanlustig.com/argentina-venture-capital-overview/.

REFERENCES

Aghion, Philippe, Peter Howitt, and Susanne Prantl. 2012. "Patent Rights, Product Market Reforms, and Innovation." Harvard University, Cambridge, MA.

Almeida, Paul, and Bruce Kogut. 1997. "The Exploration of Technological Diversity and the Geographic Localization of Innovation." *Small Business Economics* 9 (1): 21–31.

Arza, Valeria, Xavier Cirera, Augustina Colonna, and Emanuel Lopez. 2020. "Explaining Differences in the Returns to R&D in Argentina." Policy Research Working Paper 9219, World Bank, Washington, DC.

Baumol, William, J. 2002. *The Free-Market Innovation Machine: Analyzing the Growth Miracle of Capitalism*. Princeton, NJ: Princeton University Press.

Bloom, Nicholas. 2007. "Uncertainty and the Dynamics of R&D." *American Economic Review* 97 (2): 250–55.

Bond, Robert, Alex Kutsenko, and Natasha Lozitskaya. 2010. "Financial Literacy and Awareness in Ukraine: Facts and Findings." Report of the USAID Financial Sector Development Project (FINREP), US Agency for International Development, Washington, DC.

Bosch, Mariano, Daniel Lederman, and William F. Maloney. 2005. "Patenting and Research and Development: A Global View." Policy Research Working Paper 3739, World Bank, Washington, DC.

BPI France. 2018. "Hello Tomorrow lance le programme Deeptech Founders en partenariat avec Bpifrance." Press release, April 10. 2019. https://presse.bpifrance.fr/hello-tomorrow-lance-leprogramme-deeptech-founders-en-partenariat-avec-bpifrance.

Castro, Lucio, Bernardo Diaz de Astarloa, Mariana Guido, and Leonardo Iacovone. 2021. "Management in Argentina." Background paper, World Bank, Washington, DC.

Cirera, Xavier, and William F. Maloney. 2017. *The Innovation Paradox*. Washington, DC: World Bank.

Cornell University, INSEAD, and WIPO (World Intellectual Property Organization). 2018. *The Global Innovation Index 2018: Energizing the World with Innovation*. Ithaca: Cornell University; Fontainebleau: INSEAD; Geneva: WIPO.

Eurostat. 2019. Real Effective Exchange Rate (database). Brussels: European Commission. https://ec.europa.eu/eurostat/web/products-datasets/.

Fago, Vincent. 2018. "Bpifrance et Hello Tomorrow forment des chercheurs à l'entrepreneuriat." *Le Monde*, April 9, 2018.

Hall, Bronwyn H., Jacques Mairesse, and Pierre Mohnen. 2009. "Measuring the Returns to R&D." NBER Working Paper 15622, National Bureau of Economic Research, Cambridge, MA.

Jaruzelski, Barry, Robert Chwalik, and Brad Goehle. 2018. "What the Top Innovators Get Right: Global Innovation 1000 Study." *Tech and Innovation* 93 (Winter): n.p.

Maloney, William F., and Mauricio Sarrias. 2017. "Convergence to the Management Frontier." *Journal of Economic Behavior and Organization* 134 (C): 284–306.

Mulkay, Benoit, Bronwyn H. Hall, and Jacques Mairesse. 2000. "Firm-Level Investment and R&D in France and the United States: A Comparison." NBER Working Paper 8038, National Bureau of Economic Research, Cambridge, MA.

OECD (Organisation for Economic Co-operation and Development). 2014. "OECD Stat: Science Technology and Patents; Comparative Performance of National Science and Innovation Systems." OECD, Paris.

OECD (Organisation for Economic Co-operation and Development). 2016. "No Country for Young Firms? Policy Failures and Regulations Are a Greater Obstacle for Start-ups Than for Incumbents." STI Policy Note, OECD, Paris.

WEF (World Economic Forum). 2018. *The Global Competitiveness Report 2018*. Geneva: WEF.

World Bank. 2005. *Turkey Investment Climate Survey 2005: From Crisis to Private Sector Led Growth*. Washington, DC: World Bank.

World Bank. 2017. World Bank Enterprise Survey (database). Washington, DC: World Bank.

World Bank. 2019a. "Argentina Systematic Country Diagnosis, 2019." World Bank, Washington, DC.

World Bank. 2019b. "Benchmarking Argentina's Integration with the Global Economy." World Bank, Washington, DC, May 2019.

World Bank. 2019c. World Development Indicators (database). Washington, DC: World Bank.

Zucker, Lynne G., Michael R. Darby, and Yusheng Peng. 1998. "Fundamentals or Population Dynamics and the Geographic Distribution of U.S. Biotechnology Enterprises, 1976–1989." NBER Working Paper 6414, National Bureau of Economic Research, Cambridge, MA.

3 Public Expenditure Review of Innovation Policies in Argentina

This chapter analyzes the policy response to the main innovation challenges in Argentina by examining the current science, technology, and innovation (STI) policy portfolio and the corresponding budgets for 2017–18. The objective is to assess the magnitude, appropriateness, and coherence of the STI system in addressing key innovation gaps. To this end, the chapter builds on the innovation function and analysis in chapter 2.[1]

This chapter compares Argentina's innovation policy priorities with the current set of STI policy instruments. The analysis encompasses policy instruments and thus goes beyond what would normally be part of a typical public expenditure review (PER). Using this approach allows for a wider analysis than would be possible using expenditure data alone, especially since innovation and many business-related items are not categorized within the government's budget classifications. We analyze three typologies of instruments that fall under the category "transfers to firms": (a) forgone fiscal revenue due to tax incentives; (b) direct transfers to firms, including grants and matching grants; and (c) other indirect transfers to firms, including advisory support and subsidized access to credit. The PER analysis uses these data to evaluate the coherence between policy priorities and the actual policy portfolio and to assess internal consistency within the policy mix to come up with recommendations on how to improve the composition of the policy mix.

The database is constructed using the Registro de Subsidios e Incentivos created by the Ministry of Production (MoP) and lists all available STI instruments. Although this analysis is not exhaustive, the PER focuses on 216 active instruments, constituting a fairly comprehensive representation of the 2016–18 policy mix at the national level. Tax incentives are analyzed separately since they are based on estimates of forgone revenues as opposed to direct spending.

The analysis focuses on both the number of policy instruments and the total value of spending. Of the 216 active instruments, budget data are available for only 103 instruments.[2] The total budget for STI-related functions represented 0.37 percent of the total budget and 0.08 percent of gross domestic product (GDP) in 2018. A full description of the methodology used is provided in appendix C and in World Bank (2019).

OVERVIEW OF STI POLICY MIX

Argentina's investments in science, technology, and innovation have remained a residual part of public policy expenditure over the past decade. Overall public investment in innovation inputs and knowledge activities, as defined in chapter 2 of this report, have been given low priority. Between 2007 and 2015, the budget for STI policies grew along with the national budget (figure 3.1), remaining stable at 1.5 percent of the total national budget. However, this percentage was reduced to 1.1 percent in 2018 (figure 3.2).

FIGURE 3.1

Total and STI budget as a percentage of GDP in Argentina, 2007–18

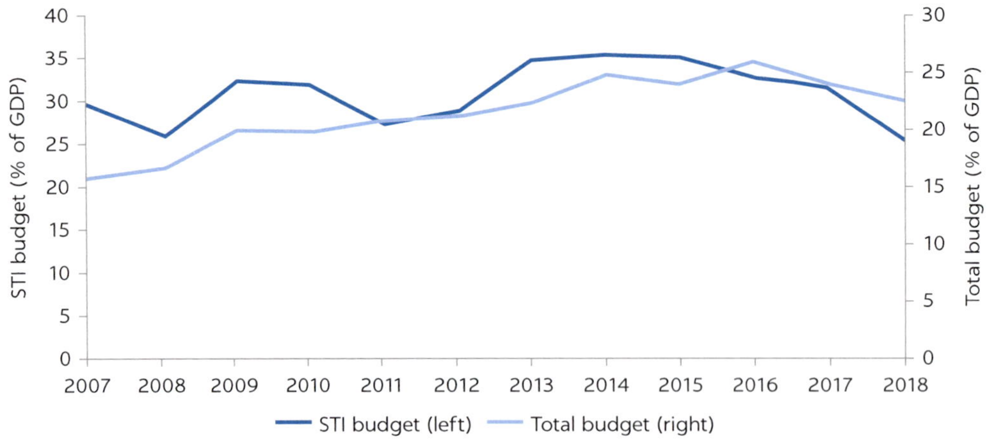

Source: World Bank 2019.
Note: GDP = gross domestic product; STI = science, technology, and innovation.

FIGURE 3.2

Public expenditure on STI as a percentage of the total budget in Argentina, 2018

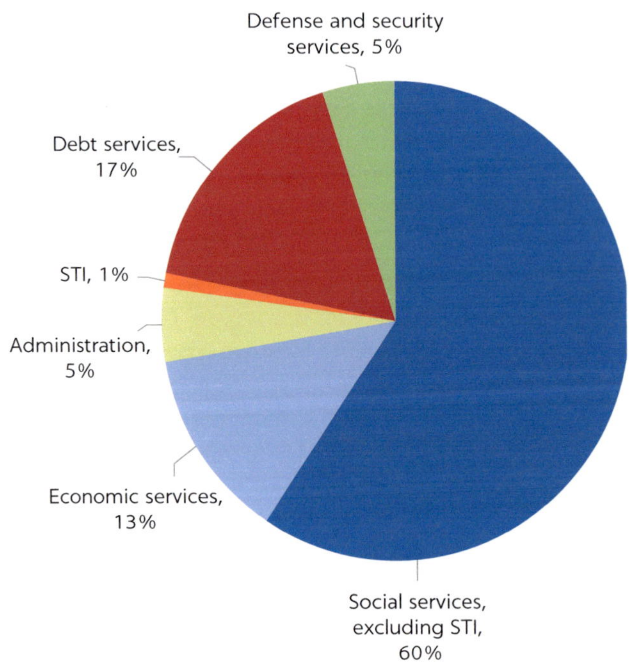

Source: World Bank 2019.
Note: STI = science, technology, and innovation.

Policy reversals undermine the medium- to long-term objectives for STI. Frequent institutional changes within and among key STI institutions have generated policy volatility and unpredictability since 2003. Predictability and stability of the relevant institutions and policies play a critical role in enabling sustainable innovation efforts. Since 2003, Argentina's STI policies have been under the purview of 10 to 20 institutions, distributed among 12 government areas and subject to three major reorganizations from 2016 to 2018 alone (figure 3.3). The Ministry of Science, Technology, and Productive Innovation (MINCyT), a key STI actor, was moved under the Ministry of Education during this time, 2016 to 2018 (it has been returned to a Ministerial position in 2019).

Three ministries manage most STI policy instruments, with the MoP, Ministry of Agribusiness, and MINCyT accounting for 73 percent of all instruments (figure 3.4) and most of the budget. Figure 3.5 uses available budget data to show the concentration of total funding over time. A small number of instruments absorb most of the budget. While the exact concentration is likely overestimated due to limited budget data, the trend remains representative.

The distribution of direct expenditures across the ministries is described in figure 3.6 (2018 data). The Ministry of Agribusiness receives the largest share of the budget, followed by the MINCyT; the MoP accounts for only 5 percent of expenditures. Based on tax incentives, however, the MoP accounts for 72 percent of forgone revenues, followed by the Ministry of Energy and Mining and the Ministry of Finance, which account for 17 percent and 11 percent, respectively.

Most of the budget is absorbed by relatively few policy instruments. The top five instruments in the MoP, Ministry of Agribusiness, and MINCyT account for 85 percent, 83 percent, and 75 percent of the relevant budget. The remaining instruments may be underfunded or surviving by inertia. Figure 3.7 segments the budget by policy instrument, with panel a showing the segmentation based on direct support and panel b showing it based on tax incentives. Within the MoP,

FIGURE 3.3

Changes in the institutional landscape in support of science, technology, and innovation, 2003–18

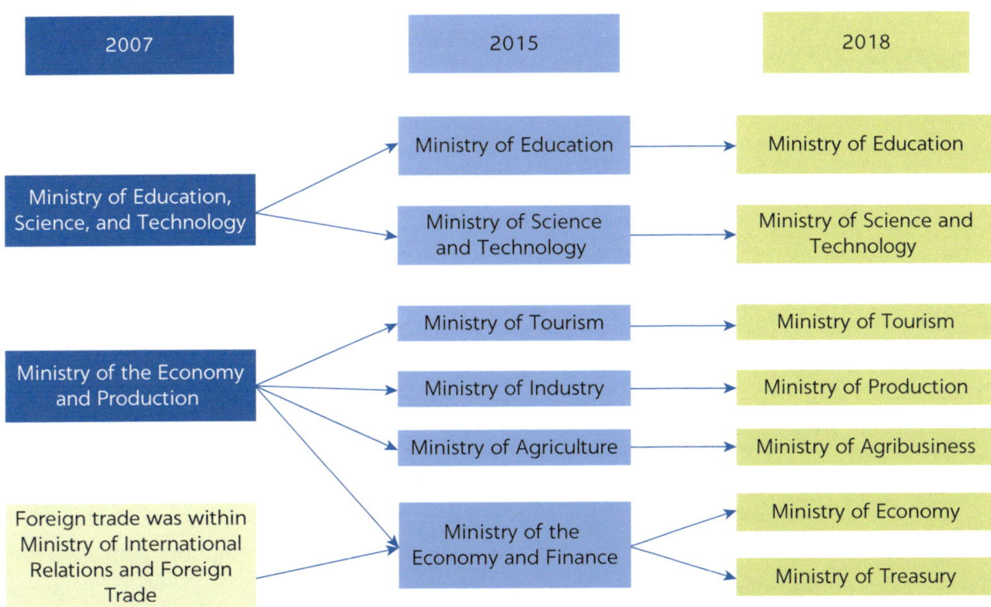

Source: World Bank 2019.

FIGURE 3.4

Share of spending for all STI instruments in Argentina, by ministry

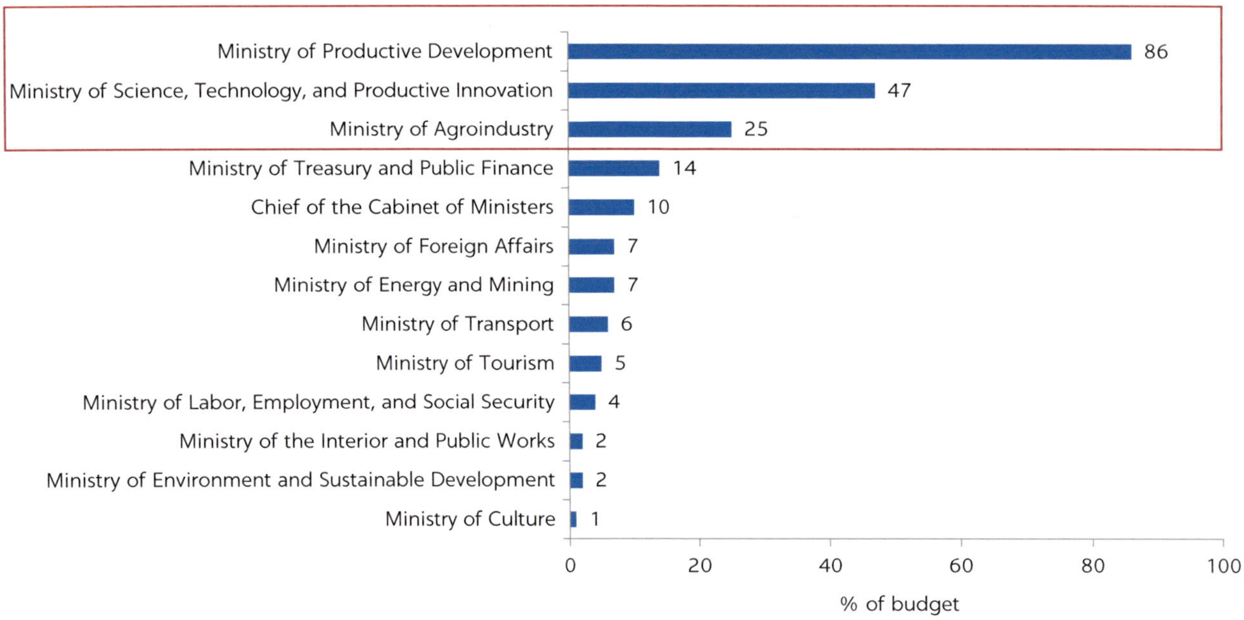

Source: World Bank 2019.
Note: STI = science, technology, and innovation.

FIGURE 3.5

Concentration of total funding, including tax incentives, in Argentina, 2012–18

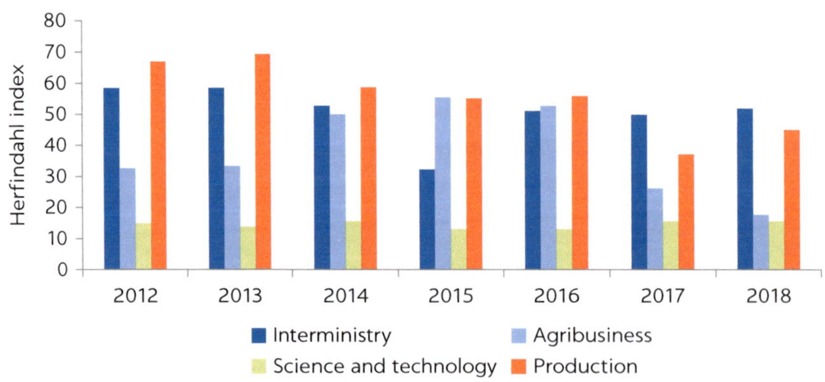

Source: World Bank 2019.
Note: The Herfindahl scores for "interministry" indicate the budget concentration between ministries. The Herfindahl scores for all other categories indicate budget concentration among instruments inside each of these ministries.

85 percent of the budget for direct support is allocated to the Supplier Development Program, the Mentors Web, the Market in Your Neighborhood, the Small and Medium Enterprises (SMEs) Experts Program, and the National Design Plan.[3] The five most important instruments that use tax incentives are the Tierra del Fuego special tax regime, the tax benefit for capital goods, SMEs investment support, car parts promotion, and SMEs promotion (explained further in box 3.1), which absorb 96 percent of the budget for this type of instrument within the Ministry of Production (figure 3.7, panel b). Of these, the first two account for 72 percent of the relevant budget.

FIGURE 3.6
Share of the budget, by ministry

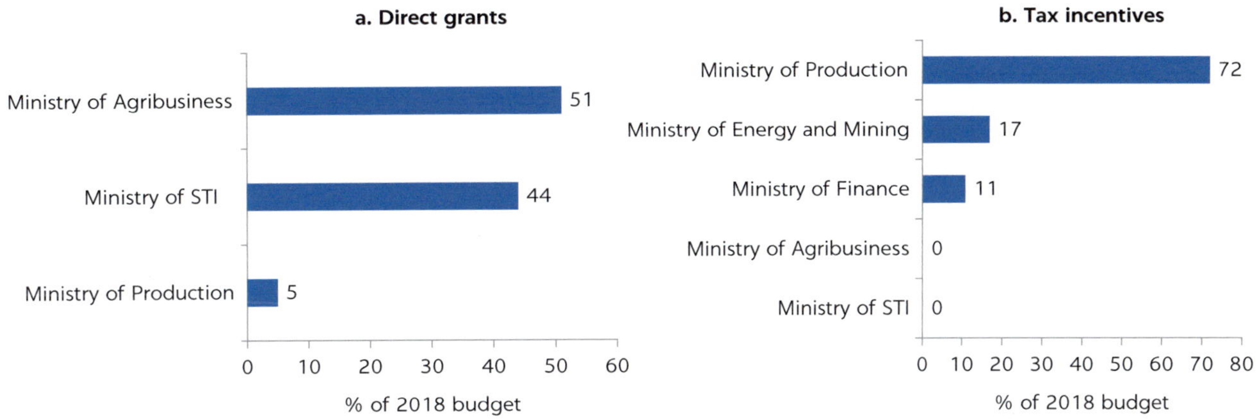

Source: World Bank 2019.
Note: STI = science, technology, and innovation.

FIGURE 3.7
Policy instruments used within the Ministry of Production, 2018

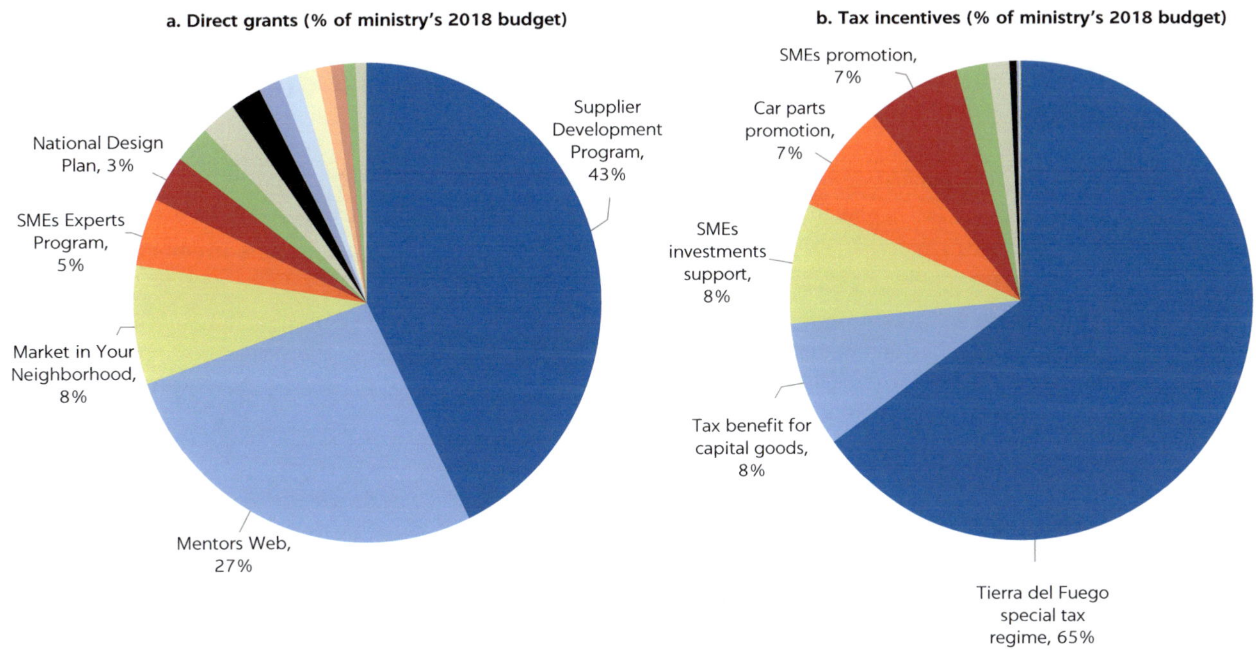

Source: Ministry of Production, Argentina.
Note: SMEs = small and medium enterprises.

Within the former Ministry of Science and Technology, four programs (each with many instruments) account for most of the STI budget: FONTAR (Argentine Technological Fund), FONCyT (Fund for Scientific and Technological Research), FONARSEC (Argentine Sectoral Fund), and FONSOFT (Software Industry Promotion Trust Fund).[4] Box 3.2 describes the top five instruments used across all three ministries.

BOX 3.1

The five most important policy instruments that use tax incentives: Summary description

- *The Tierra del Fuego special tax regime* exempts firms from paying various taxes in order to promote industry and establish population in the southern extreme of the country.
- *Biofuel's sustainable use and consumption regime* aims to generate technological innovation in the biofuels area by lowering the value added and income taxes on capital goods and infrastructure works. The ultimate objective is to extend the use of biofuels to different economic sectors and bring about a reduction in the environmental footprint.
- *Strengthening SMEs regime* gives a distinct tax treatment to small and medium enterprises as part of a larger program targeting firms in crisis.
- *The national fabrication of capital goods regime* benefits the manufacturers of capital goods with tax discounts for sales made inside the national territory.
- *SMEs investment support* seeks to encourage investments in capital goods and infrastructure by lowering the value added and income taxes of small and medium firms.

BOX 3.2

The five most important policy instruments that use direct support: Summary description

- *The Scientific and Technological Research Projects Program (PICT-PICTO, part of FONCyT)* includes three instruments (PICT, PICTO, and PICT Start-Up). PICT gives direct grants to public or nonprofit institutions for research and development projects. PICTO cofinances in equal parts public-private partnerships for research and development projects of common interest, and PICT Start-Up funds groups that transform existing knowledge into products or services that address a societal or market need.
- *The Sugar Sector Competitiveness Program* provides credit for industry located in the Northwest region of the country, especially for the sustainable production of ethanol and the support of small producers.
- *The Provincial Agricultural Services Program* gives grants and direct support for infrastructure to implement different programs oriented to improve agricultural and food services, considering social and environmental sustainability.
- *The National System for the Prevention and Mitigation of Agricultural Emergencies and Disasters* awards grants to diminish the impact of climate adversity on agricultural production, which can be used to reconstruct productive infrastructure, to install protection systems, and the like.
- *The second article of the promotional benefit of Law no. 23.877 (part of FONTAR)* gives credit to small and medium enterprises to improve their products and update their machinery.

OBJECTIVES AND THE MOST COMMONLY USED INSTRUMENTS IN THE STI POLICY MIX

Most beneficiaries of STI support in Argentina are formal, mature SMEs. Formal firms, state-owned enterprises, and cooperatives are the most frequent beneficiaries of STI support, with 190, 186, and 178 instruments, respectively (figure 3.8), targeting them. Since all types of firms are eligible for these instruments, this orientation indicates poor targeting of beneficiaries. Research institutes and

FIGURE 3.8
STI policy mix in Argentina, by type of beneficiaries

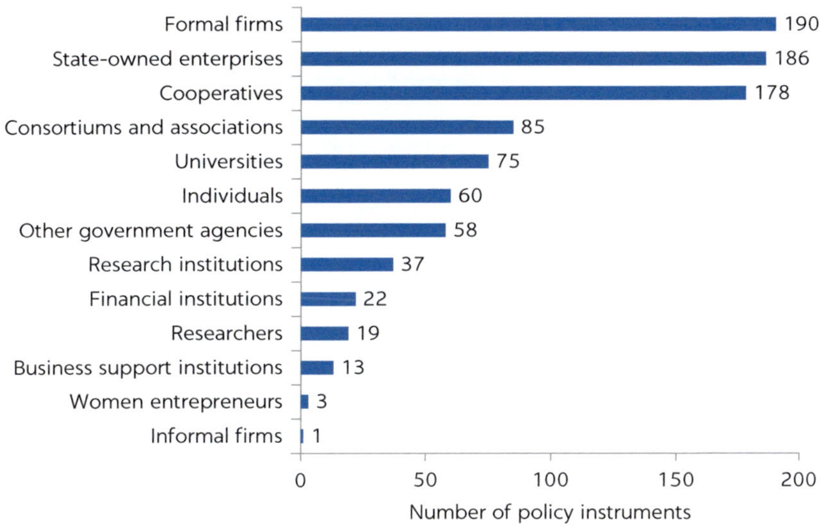

Source: World Bank 2019.
Note: Instruments often have more than one type of beneficiary, so the figure necessarily duplicates data. Appendixes C and D provide more detail on the categories. STI = science, technology, and innovation.

researchers appear in the bottom half, with fewer than 40 instruments each.[5] Only four instruments target female entrepreneurs and informal firms.

Among innovation outcomes, improving productivity is the primary stated objective, with more than 150 instruments citing higher productivity as an expected outcome (in line with government goals). Diversification is the second most cited goal, with almost 90 instruments. Knowledge creation (generating new productive knowledge) and environment and climate change (reducing the environmental footprint or improving the management of natural resources) follow, at 50 instruments each. Non-R&D innovation is the most common secondary objective for individual instruments (85), followed by skills formation (61) and improvement in management practices (57). The next positions are occupied by business R&D, domestic market, and export promotion. Particularly worrisome is the low priority given to export promotion. This is contrary to stated policy objectives, especially the second place accorded to economic diversification as a societal outcome pursued by the government.

SMEs receive most support, although a significant number of programs are directed at large companies (figure 3.9, panel a). Most instruments focus on consolidated or growing ventures rather than start-ups (figure 3.9, panel b). Firms are selected according to their growth potential, but no preference is given to high-tech firms. Almost half of the programs are oriented at projects identified as having high growth potential and as being potential innovators (71). Support for R&D-intensive (58) and technology-intensive (52) projects is less frequent. The STI policy mix shows a clear preference for firms that do not innovate regularly but have the potential to do so, ruling out those that already do it and those that never do it (figure 3.10, panel a).

Among innovation inputs, most grants are used to purchase machinery and equipment, with 68 instruments used to this end, followed by R&D, with 38 instruments (figure 3.10, panel b). Grants are most effective at addressing capability and coordination failures, which are discussed in more detail in

FIGURE 3.9
STI instruments, by firm size and life cycle

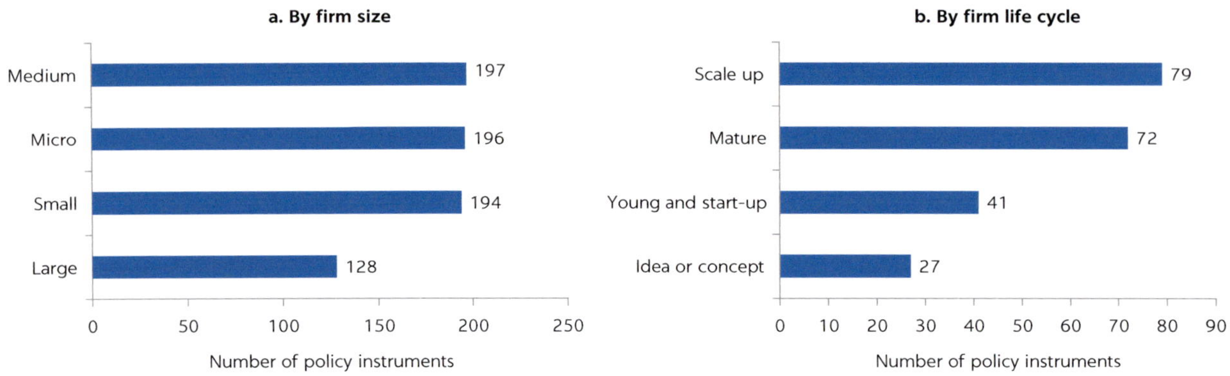

Source: World Bank 2019.
Note: STI = science, technology, and innovation.

FIGURE 3.10
STI instruments, by grant potential and use

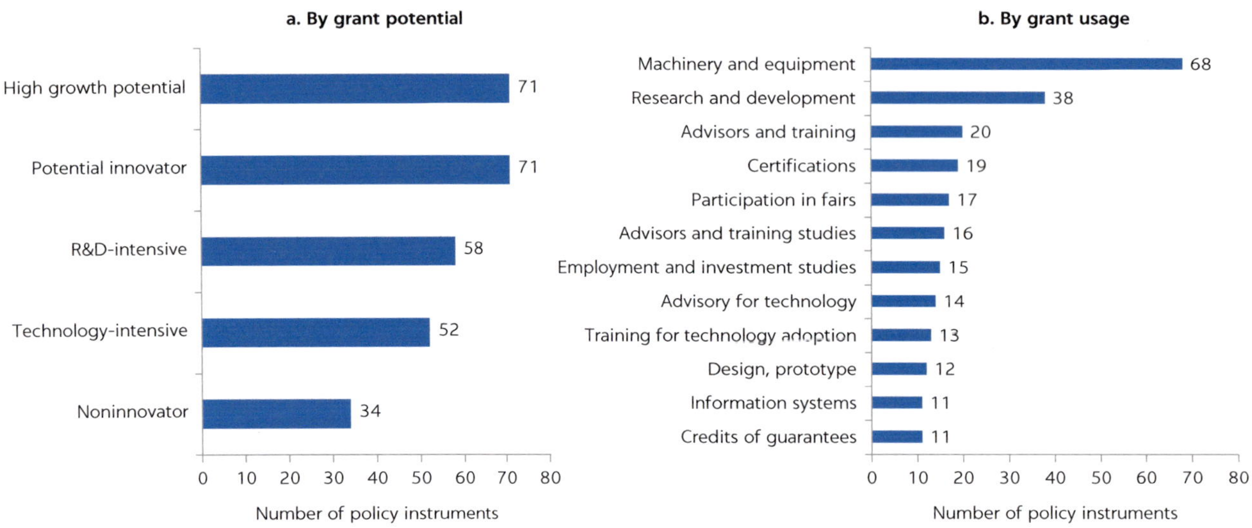

Source: World Bank 2019.
Note: R&D = research and development; STI = science, technology, and innovation.

box 3.3. Box 3.4 discusses loans and loan guarantees. Given the current fiscal consolidation and the reduced amount of resources available for grants, prioritizing these types of activities is of critical importance. Moreover, since machinery and equipment are assets, these programs would be better supported with lending programs that include a subsidy or guarantee to address the risk and moral hazard of market failures associated with them.

Finally, Argentina overly relies on tax incentives to support STI investments in the private sector. Tax incentives are generally tailored to compensate for externalities, but they are not always the most appropriate instrument to use for supporting innovation (box 3.5 provides additional detail) when the problem is, for example, related to lack of capabilities or imperfect financing. Tax incentives make up an increasingly large share of total spending across STI instruments in Argentina (figure 3.11). Even excluding major programs such as

BOX 3.3

When and how best to use grants and matching grants for financing innovation

Grants and matching grants are the most common form of direct government support to firms for both research and development (R&D) and non-R&D activities. On average, high-income countries spend more on direct government support than on indirect support. In 2013, Organisation for Economic Co-operation and Development (OECD) member states invested approximately US$40 billion in direct government funding for business R&D, equivalent to 6.9 percent of business R&D, while publicly funded indirect measures, such as R&D tax incentives, represented approximately 5.2 percent of business R&D (Appelt et al. 2016). Similarly, 80 percent of OECD countries had matching grant schemes in 2010, while 66 percent had tax incentive programs; 45 percent of all countries used both instruments. Such programs were less common in Latin America, where 65 percent of the countries used matching grants and only 30 percent used tax incentives (Benavente et al. 2012).

Matching grants address a variety of market failures, including (a) positive externalities and spillovers, wherein the benefits of R&D and non-R&D-based innovation are captured by firms in addition to the firm conducting the research or innovation; (b) coordination failures, wherein the high barriers and costs to coordination or cooperation among firms can be overcome with a matching-grant structure; (c) capability failures, wherein some firms (often small and medium enterprises) lack the knowledge, skills, or expertise to innovate; and (d) capital market failures, wherein financial markets cannot price and respond appropriately to the funding needs of medium- to long-term investments.

Global experience suggests that successful grant programs are simple and easy to understand, with clear eligibility criteria and application processes, a transparent and timely selection process, and efficient grant disbursement processes. Such programs are also generally competitive, with international experts involved in selection. Meta-analyses from Becker (2015), García-Quevedo (2004), and Zúñiga-Vicente et al. (2014) conclude that most grant schemes do not result in crowding-out effects, while some result in crowding-in effects, especially in the context of emerging economies (for example, as noted in Özçelik and Taymaz 2008). However, the type of firm and economic segment or sector targeted and features of their design (for example, competitive selection) affect the degree and type of impact.

Direct grant support can be particularly valuable for smaller and younger firms, which often do not generate taxable income from innovation-related projects for years. Such firms benefit from horizontal support such as tax credits only if there are complex carryover or credit provisions. Evaluations in OECD countries suggest that tax incentives increase R&D spending only in firms already investing in R&D; they do not encourage firms with no previous R&D investments (Dechezleprêtre et al. 2016; Veugelers 2016). Similarly, Busom (1999) finds that grants are better suited than tax incentives to encouraging young, knowledge-based firms to engage in R&D in Spain; Benavente et al. (2012) suggest that grant schemes are more effective at encouraging new innovators and stimulating collaborations in Latin America. Moreover, González and Pazó (2008), Herrera and Bravo Ibarra (2010), and Lee and Cin (2010) suggest that supporting smaller firms with grant schemes is more effective than subsidizing large firms. In the same vein, based on a study of approximately 12,000 firms in 30 Eastern European and Central Asian countries, Mateut (2018) finds that R&D and innovation activities are higher among young firms that receive grants or subsidies. This finding is particularly true in financially constrained firms.

Studies also show that competitive grants outperform entitlement-based grants, although both are subject to selection bias. Caloffi et al. (2018) find that collaboration grants (which encourage cooperation between two or more actors) should increase the number of R&D-producing small and medium enterprises. That said, individual grants tend to work better over time for incentivizing or inducing R&D input additionality (that is, making R&D investments). Studies in Argentina also suggest that grant programs have positive effects. Hall and Maffioli (2008) find that both FONTEC (Argentine Technological Entrepreneurship Fund) and FONTAR (Argentine Technological Fund) positively affected firm growth in terms of both employment (3.1 percent for FONTEC and 1.5 percent for FONTAR) and sales (39.6 percent for FONTEC and 1.5 percent for FONTAR), after a two-year lag. Álvarez (2016) find that FONTEC boosted employment by 6.4 percent and wages by 4.6 percent.

BOX 3.4

When and how best to use loans and loan guarantees for financing innovation

Innovation loans are publicly supported lending instruments, managed either directly by the government or indirectly through a financial intermediary (such as a bank), that provide financing for innovation investments. Such loans can also be supported by guarantee schemes, often backed by governments, which take first losses in the event of default, thereby incentivizing private sector lending. These loans often offer subsidized interest rates to account for an unpredictable cash flow profile, a high degree of assets that are intangible and difficult to collateralize, and information asymmetries.

These loans address market failures, including (a) information asymmetries between borrowers and lenders and (b) incomplete appropriability of the returns on investment, since competitor firms may also benefit from the innovation investments.

Most loans require full repayment regardless of the innovation's results (for example, whether the innovation investment leads to increased cash flows), although a smaller subset requires repayment only if the innovation succeeds. Innovation loans work well when they address a specific mismatch in the financial markets—for example, when they are tailored or targeted toward certain activities, sectors, or firm sizes—or are able to use existing financial infrastructure when governments are resource-constrained. These programs, however, are at greater risk of failure when loans are administered directly by government; they can face challenges in identifying innovative firms and difficulties in monitoring innovation outcomes. Additionally, they can create credit market distortions and crowd out the financial sector.

Özçelik and Taymaz (2008) find that innovation loans in Turkey had positive effects on research and development (R&D) spending for smaller firms and firms in technology-intensive industries. Huergo and Martín (2014) find that participation in a soft loan system for innovation funding increased self-financing of internal R&D activities by 81.8 percent compared with 76 percent for grant schemes (based on Spanish programs). Machado, Martini, and da Gama (2017) evaluate the Brazilian Development Bank's Innovation Credit Scheme and find a statistically significant positive effect on R&D expenditures. Specifically, firms supported by the Innovation Credit Scheme tended to invest at least 30 percent more in R&D than companies outside the program.

FIGURE 3.11

Resources allocated to STI instruments in Argentina's 2018 budget

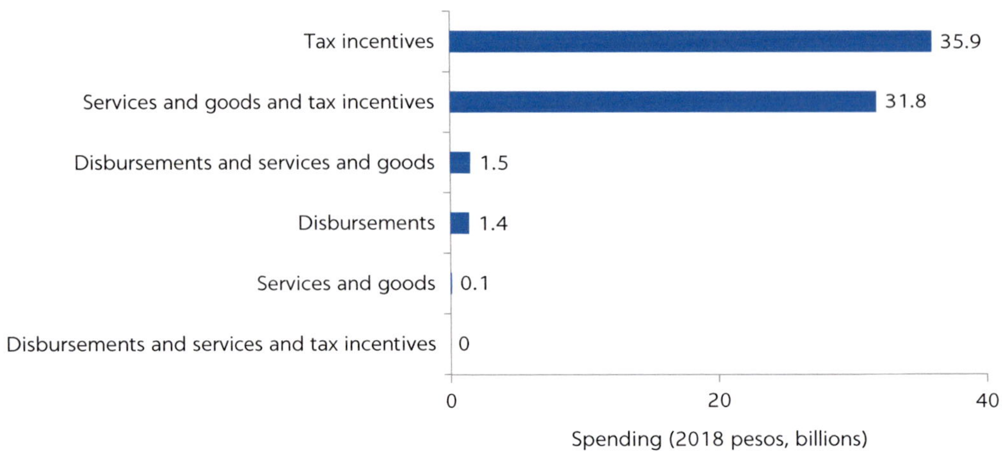

Source: World Bank 2019.
Note: STI = science, technology, and innovation.

BOX 3.5

When and how to use tax incentives for innovation

Tax incentives for research and development (R&D) reduce the tax burden of firms that invest in innovation. They address several market failures, primarily (a) incomplete appropriability, when firms underinvest because they cannot fully capture the benefits of R&D, some of which become "public" goods and benefit competitors; and (b) coordination failures, when firms are underincentivized to collaborate with universities and other research institutions.

Tax incentives primarily take two forms: (a) those based on R&D expenditures and (b) those based on R&D results. The former is more prominent globally, whereas the latter allows innovative firms to keep more of the profits resulting from innovation investments—for example, profits that come from patented technology. Despite early-stage R&D being the most risky, most schemes focus on applied research, rather than "generic" R&D, and tend to focus on reducing the tax burden associated with R&D labor, subcontracted and collaborative R&D, and materials and overhead.

Tax incentives can be based on volume (firms can deduct all R&D expenditures in a given year); incremental (firms can deduct spending above a given baseline, often from the previous year); and hybrid, which combine the two schemes. Tax incentives for incremental R&D are better suited for not crowding out private investment but are harder to enforce.

As a policy tool, tax incentives lower administrative and compliance costs and have a simpler implementation structure than direct support for firms. Beneficiaries are able to choose their projects, reducing the risk of crowding out. Tax incentives also scale well, and large firms can use them to subsidize large R&D schemes.

R&D tax breaks introduce budgetary and revenue uncertainty. Additionally, the applicability of deductions is difficult to verify, resulting in misreporting either intentionally or unintentionally. Tax incentives are poorly suited for targeting specific sectors or types of spending.

Policy makers need to consider the following five elements in designing tax incentives for R&D: (a) appropriate level of tax benefit; (b) duration of the incentive scheme—ideally long term to enable planning by firms; (c) scheme modality, for example, expenditure versus nonexpenditure and volume, incremental or hybrid approaches; (d) eligibility for deduction; and (e) specific target group, if any.

Calderón-Madrid (2011), focusing on the Mexican experience, finds that firms increased their spending by 48 cents on the dollar for every dollar they had previously spent on innovation R&D in the presence of a tax incentive. Mercer-Blackman (2008), studying Colombia, finds that an R&D-focused tax scheme generated an incremental 5 cents of additional private spending for every dollar of tax reduction. Binelli and Maffioli (2007) find that every 1 percent of forgone tax revenue generated 13.2 percent of incremental R&D spending.

Tierra del Fuego, which has objectives other than innovation, the ratio of spending for tax incentives to spending for all other instruments combined appears to be as high as 6:1.

RECENT CHANGES IN THE STI POLICY MIX

Recent trends in fiscal consolidation risk reversing the alignment of the STI policy mix with the growth and diversification agenda of Argentina. Between 2017 and 2018, funds directed at STI policies were reduced considerably. Excluding tax incentives, these budget reductions totaled approximately 64 percent. Each of the three most important STI ministries (including the Ministry of Agribusiness, MoP, and MINCyT) experienced budget reductions of more than 60 percent during this time period. Figure 3.12 provides further details on the budget reductions by ministry, and figure 3.13 on budget reductions by type of instrument (both tax incentive and nontax incentive instruments).

Between 2017 and 2018, policy has shifted away from the disbursement or provision of goods and services and toward the use of tax incentives. Although all STI policy instruments experienced budget reductions, the relative portion of tax incentives within the mix of instruments expanded considerably. If we look at the budget excluding tax incentives, the reduction in the budget was around 64 percent. The three most important STI ministries—the Ministry of Agribusiness, MoP, and MINCyT—had a budget reduction of 62 percent (aggregated average) between 2017 and 2018 (figure 3.12, panel a). Although the value of tax incentive programs can be easily overestimated, when tax incentives are included, the three primary STI ministries show a combined budget reduction of only 19 percent, with the Ministry of Agribusiness, MINCyT, and MoP experiencing budget reductions of 69 percent, 47 percent, and 18 percent, respectively (figure 3.12, panel b).

All policy instruments targeted at productivity growth and better innovation outcomes also suffered recent budget cuts, although the extent of these cuts varied across the instruments (figure 3.13). Non-R&D instruments and those oriented toward managerial practices experienced lighter reductions. Similarly, machinery purchases also received lower relative cuts, along with economic advice and prototype design. Support for obtaining certifications declined significantly, despite being an important facet of regulating competition both internally and internationally (figure 3.14, panels a and b). This reduction conflicts

FIGURE 3.12

Budget changes, by ministry, 2017–18

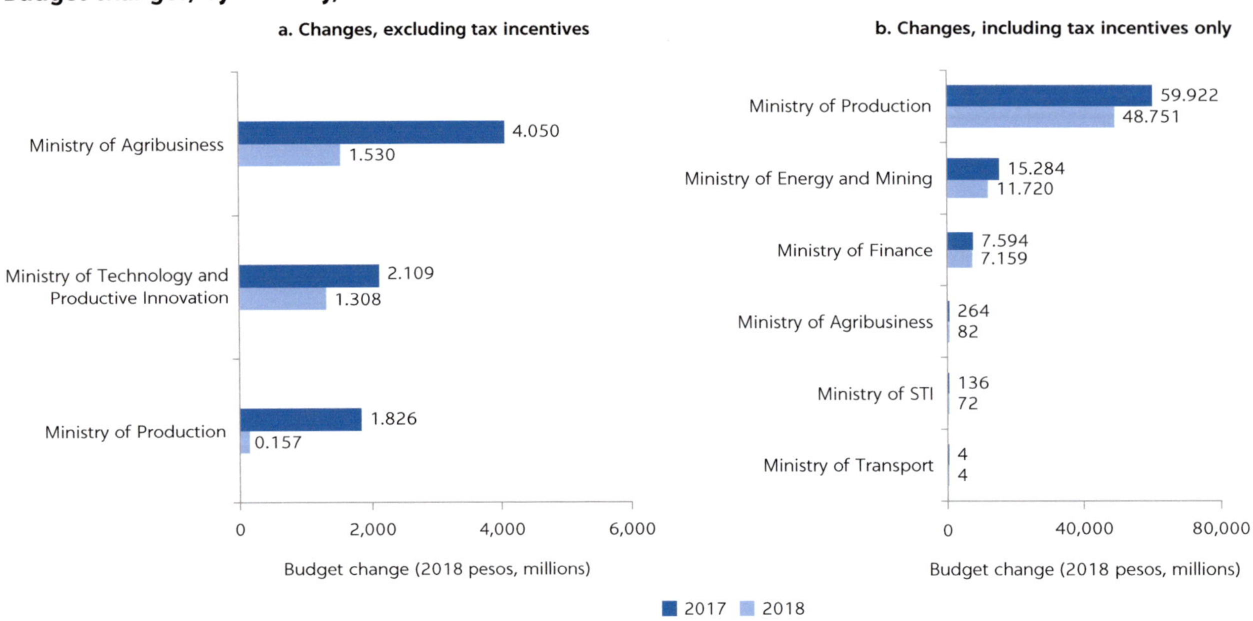

Source: World Bank 2019.
Note: STI = science, technology, and innovation.

FIGURE 3.13
Budget reduction, by type of STI instrument, 2017–18

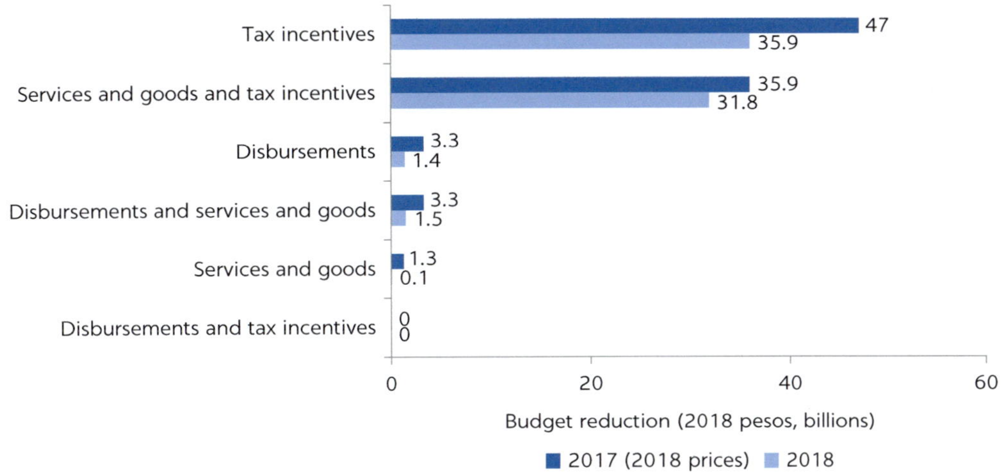

Source: World Bank 2019.
Note: STI = science, technology, and innovation.

FIGURE 3.14
Budget changes in Argentina, by objective and grant use, 2017–18

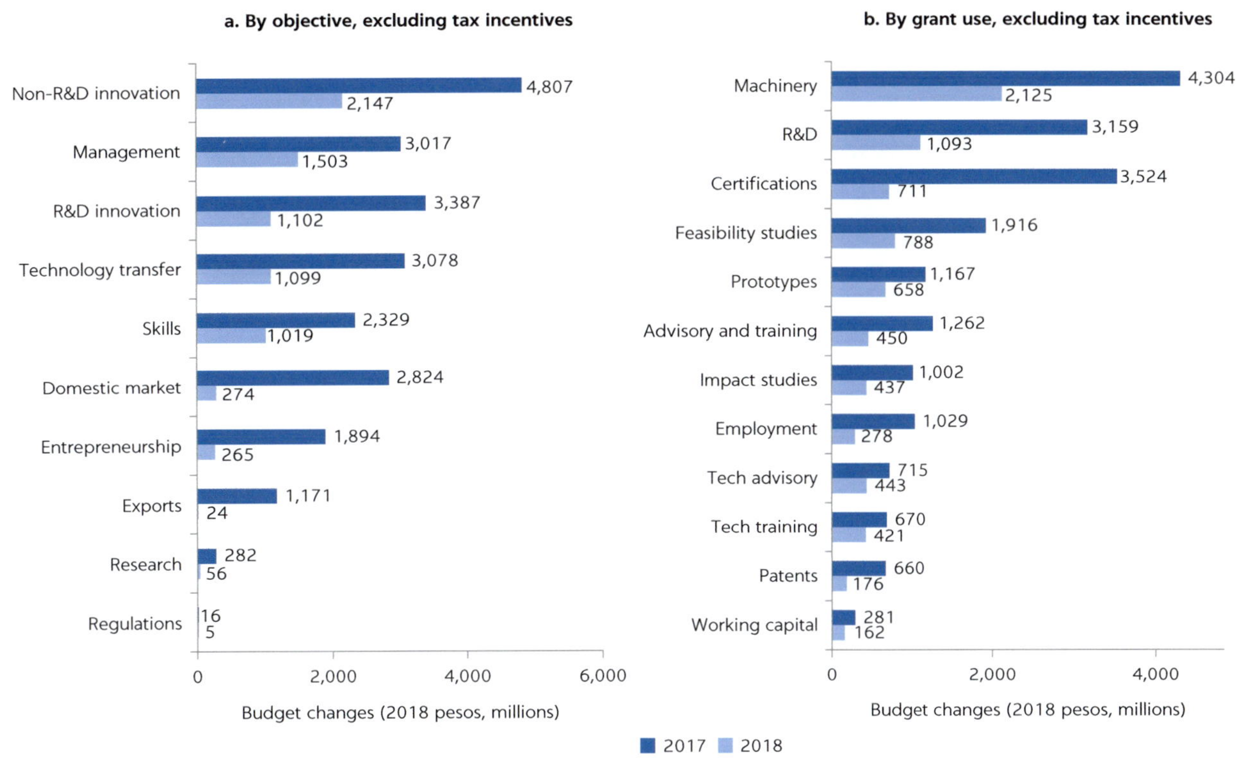

Source: World Bank 2019.
Note: R&D = research and development.

FIGURE 3.15
Budget changes in Argentina, by firm life cycle, 2017–18

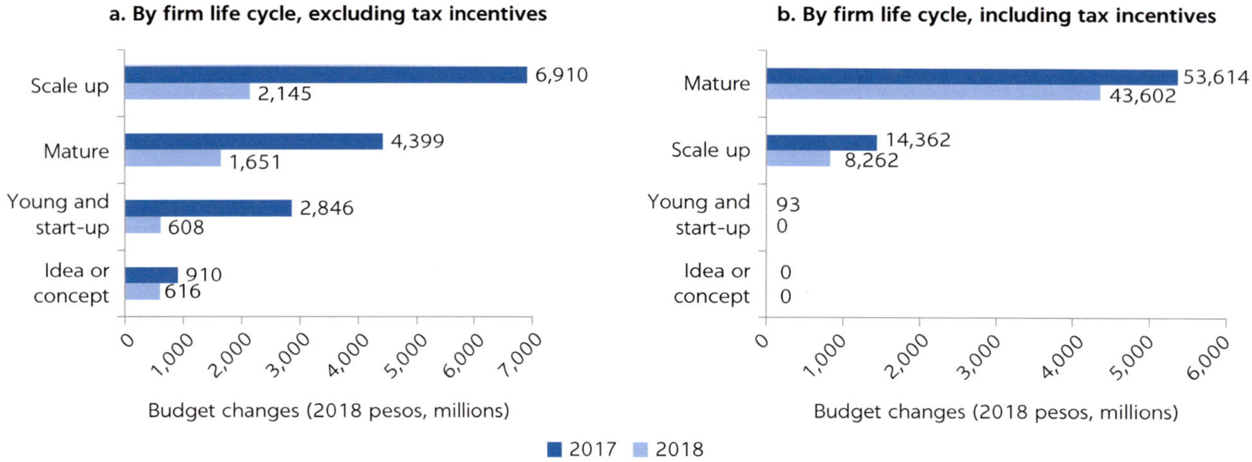

Source: World Bank 2019.
Note: R&D = research and development.

with stated government priorities to promote domestic competition and foster export competitiveness.

Policy objectives related to improving innovation inputs in terms of R&D, knowledge creation, and skills, as well as policies aimed at improving innovation outcomes and impacts, such as market access, diversification, entrepreneurship, and export promotion, suffered the largest cuts. At 98 percent, export promotion received the largest cut, followed by entrepreneurship (86 percent) and research excellence (80 percent). These budget reductions also contrast with government priorities to increase exports, promote new business, and promote links between business and science.

Programs directed at mature and scaling-up firms also retained a higher proportion of funding relative to start-ups and younger firms. Young and start-up firms experienced the most significant relative cutback, at 79 percent (figure 3.15). Along with idea-stage firms, these types of firms received minimal support.

KEY FINDINGS

There is significant room for improving the coherence of the STI policy mix. Argentina's pro–market reform agenda has focused on reducing public expenditures and deficits, improving efficiency, promoting domestic competition and international integration, federalizing production, and facilitating the creation of formal employment. Good progress has been made, but some important inconsistencies and unfinished rebalancing of the policy mix constrain the impact of STI policies. These inconsistencies are summarized as follows.

Recent fiscal consolidation has disproportionately affected key government priorities. Since mid-2000s, government started to reorient the STI policy mix toward the innovation side, with firms playing a central role in STI strategy. The strategy also anchored policies to enhance export competitiveness as a key driver of growth and recognized the importance of improving managerial practices as an important building block for an effective STI system. These are important steps toward improving the mix of policies. Nevertheless, the fiscal consolidation of 2017–18 disproportionately affected some of these key objectives and risked reversing some of these gains. While the overall budget reduction is consistent with the government's aim to reduce public expenditures and the public deficit, the relatively high reduction in budget for STI is inconsistent with the government's goal of developing the productive sector. For example, cutbacks in the already limited STI policies that support exports are not consistent with the government's aims to improve Argentina's position in global markets. Such cutbacks could undermine STI in the long term, weakening an important foundational piece of long-term growth.

The STI institutional landscape is characterized by shifting priorities and fragmentation, resulting in economic uncertainty and hindering firm investments. Institutional changes indicate that recent policy changes are not aligned with improving productivity growth. While reducing the number of instruments could reduce complexity and bureaucracy, such changes increase economic uncertainty. The inclusion of MINCyT under the Ministry of Education and away from the MoP during this time (2016–18) also does not align science and technology policy with productive activities.

Tax incentives have become the primary STI policy instrument for supporting private sector innovation in Argentina, but market failures continue to weaken innovation investments and performance. Incumbents already investing in R&D benefit automatically from tax incentives, while new entrants and early-stage innovators do not. Additionally, tax incentives generally do not directly support firms' absorptive capacity, which is a key constraint to innovation in Argentina.

Current STI policies are not focused on creating linkages and collaboration between science and industry, resulting in large inefficiencies in innovation. Promoting linkages with research institutions should be prioritized. This effort would support science and development activities and direct partnerships between scientific activities and production actors. Few STI instruments are targeted at promoting collaboration of scientists and firms and the creation of spinoffs.

Access to STI policy data is fragmented and ad hoc, and increasing the transparency and accessibility of data are an important part of building an evidence-based STI decision-making and monitoring process. For example, in the context of this analysis, we encountered several difficulties in obtaining the data—signaling issues in transparency for the evaluation of public policy.

NOTES

1. For a full description of the methodology, see Correa (2014).
2. We use data from Open Budget and are confident that most instruments in policies for production, innovation, and entrepreneurship are designed and implemented by the ministries from which we requested data. However, we managed to collect budget data for only 26 percent of the amount of transfers for STI-related functions by these ministries in 2018.
3. The Supplier Development Program and the Mentors Web account for 70 percent of the ministry's budget for these types of instruments. The Supplier Development Program offers grants, technical assistance, and credit benefits for some strategic sectors of manufacturing and mining industries with the intention of promoting national suppliers and diversifying the structure of production. The Mentors Web provides technical assistance through mentors who help entrepreneurs to improve their projects and create firms and jobs.

4. Each of the four programs promotes different aspects related to science and technology. FONTAR supports private sector productivity through technological innovation. FONCyT endorses R&D projects that generate new scientific knowledge. FONARSEC promotes activities and projects that transfer knowledge to a few key sectors (especially technology-intensive ones, like agribusiness and biotechnology). FONSOFT focuses on the information, communications, and technology sector, supporting the finalization of degrees, creation of firms, and strengthening of SMEs.
5. The main agency supporting research—the National Scientific and Technical Research Council (CONICET)—and most instruments in FONCyT supporting basic science are excluded from our analysis. We include only instruments that support research funded and administered by other institutions.

REFERENCES

Álvarez, Roberto. 2016. "The Impact of R&D and ICT Investment on Innovation and Productivity in Chilean Firms." Working Paper wp428, University of Chile, Department of Economics, Santiago.

Appelt, Silvia, Matej Bajgar, Chiara Criscuolo, and Fernando Galindo-Rueda. 2016. "R&D Tax Incentives: Evidence on Design, Incidence, and Impacts." OECD Science, Technology and Industry Policy Paper 32, Organisation for Economic Co-operation and Development (OECD) Publishing, Paris. https://doi.org/10.1787/5jlr8fldqk7j-en.

Becker, Bettina. 2015. "Public R&D Policies and Private R&D Investment: A Survey of the Empirical Evidence." *Journal of Economic Surveys* 29 (5): 917–42.

Benavente, José, Gustavo Crespi, Lucas Figal Garone, and Alessandro Maffioli. 2012. "The Impact of National Research Funds: A Regression Discontinuity Approach to the Chilean FONDECYT." *Research Policy* 41 (8): 1461–75. doi:10.1016/j.respol.2012.04.007.

Binelli, Chiara, and Alessandro Maffioli. 2007. "A Micro-econometric Analysis of Public Support to Private R&D in Argentina." *International Review of Applied Economics* 21 (3): 339–59. 10.1080/02692170701390320.

Busom, Isabel. 1999. "An Empirical Evaluation of the Effects of R&D Subsidies." Burch Working Paper B99-05, University of California, Berkeley.

Calderón-Madrid, Angel. 2011. "A Micro-Econometric Analysis of the Impact of Mexico's R&D Tax Credit Program on Private R&D Expenditure." Working Paper, El Colegio de México, Mexico City. Paper presented at the 3IE (International Initiative for Impact Evaluation) international conference, "Mind the Gap: From Evidence to Policy Impact," Cuernavaca, México, June 15–17, 2011.

Caloffi, Annalisa, Marco Mariani, Federica Rossi, and Margherita Russo. 2018. "A Comparative Evaluation of Regional Subsidies for Collaborative and Individual R&D in Small and Medium-Sized Enterprises." *Research Policy* 47 (8): 1437–47.

Correa, Paulo. 2014. "Public Expenditure Reviews in Science, Technology, and Innovation: A Guidance Note." World Bank, Washington, DC.

Dechezleprêtre, Antoine, Elias Einiö, Ralf Martin, Kieu-Trang Nguyen, and John Van Reenen. 2016. "Do Tax Incentives for Research Increase Firm Innovation? An RD Design for R&D." GRI Working Paper 230, Grantham Research Institute on Climate Change and the Environment, London.

García-Quevedo, José. 2004. "Do Public Subsidies Complement Business R&D? A Meta-Analysis of the Econometric Evidence." *Kyklos* 57 (1): 87–102.

González, Xulia, and Consuelo Pazó. 2008. "Do Public Subsidies Stimulate Private R&D Spending?" *Research Policy* 37 (3): 371–89. doi:10.1016/j.respol.2007.10.009.

Hall, Bronwyn, and Alessandro Maffioli. 2008. "Evaluating the Impact of Technology Development Funds in Emerging Economies: Evidence from Latin America." *European Journal of Development Research* 20 (2): 172–98. doi:10.1080/09578810802060819.

Herrera, Lliana, and Edna R. Bravo Ibarra. 2010. "Distribution and Effect of R&D Subsidies: A Comparative Analysis According to Firm Size." *Intangible Capital* 6 (2): 272–99. https://www.intangiblecapital.org/index.php/ic/article/view/214.

Huergo, Elena, and Lourdes Martín. 2014. "National or International Public Funding? Subsidies or Loans? Evaluating the Innovation Impact of R&D Support Programmes." MPRA Paper 54218, Universidad Complutense de Madrid, Group for Research in Productivity, Innovation, and Competition (GRIPICO), Madrid. https://mpra.ub.uni-muenchen.de/54218/.

Lee, Eui, and Beom Cin. 2010. "The Effect of Risk-Sharing Government Subsidy on Corporate R&D Investment: Empirical Evidence from Korea." *Technological Forecasting and Social Change* 77 (6): 881–90. doi:10.1016/j.techfore.2010.01.012.

Machado, Luciano, Ricardo A. Martini, and Marina M. da Gama. 2017. "Does BNDES Innovation Credit Boost Firms' R&D Expenditures? Evidence from Brazilian Panel Data." Working Paper, Brazilian Development Bank (BNDES), Rio de Janeiro.

Mateut, Simona. 2018. "Subsidies, Financial Constraints, and Firm Innovative Activities in Emerging Economies." *Small Business Economics* 50 (1): 131–62. doi:10.1007/s11187-017-9877-3.

Mercer-Blackman, Valerie. 2008. "The Impact of Research and Development Tax Incentives on Colombia's Manufacturing Sector: What Difference Do They Make?" IMF Working Paper 08/178, International Monetary Fund, Washington, DC. https://ssrn.com/abstract=1266511.

Özçelik, Emre, and Erol Taymaz. 2008. "R&D Support Programs in Developing Countries: The Turkish Experience." *Research Policy* 37 (2): 258–75. doi:10.1016/j.respol.2007.11.001.

Veugelers, Reinhilde. 2016. "Getting the Most from Public R&D Spending in Times of Budgetary Austerity." Working Paper 13004, Bruegel, Brussels.

World Bank. 2019. "Public Expenditure Review: Policies Oriented to Support Production, Innovation, and Entrepreneurship in Argentina: Past and Present; Strengths and Challenges." Background paper for this report, World Bank, Washington, DC.

Zúñiga-Vicente, José, César Alonso-Borrego, Francisco Forcadell, and José Galán. 2014. "Assessing the Effect of Public Subsidies on Firm R&D Investment: A Survey." *Journal of Economic Surveys* 28 (1): 36–67. doi:10.1111/j.1467-6419.2012.00738.x.

4 Insights from Recent Initiatives Supporting Public-Private Partnerships and Knowledge-Based Entrepreneurship

Innovation policy in Argentina has traditionally centered on a large range of programs and interventions focused on the growth and productivity of small and medium enterprises (SMEs) and support for research and development (R&D) and academic research. According to McDermott (2000), as of 2000, approximately 300 programs and lines of credit supported SMEs alone (IAMC 1999, 23). Since the late 2000s, however, a small number of initiatives have focused more deliberately on public-private partnerships, the knowledge economy, technology-based entrepreneurships, and technology transfer. These policies have included sectoral funds (FSATs) for software and for agriculture, health, and energy as well as support for public-private partnerships, which have extended across all sectors. In this chapter, we provide highlights from results and impact evaluations of two of these recent initiatives—one supporting entrepreneurship (EMPRETECNO) and one supporting public-private partnerships in innovation (Argentine Sectoral Fund [FONARSEC]). These evaluations offer insights on the design, demand, and implementation experience of such programs in Argentina.

TECHNOLOGY-BASED ENTREPRENEURSHIP: EMPRETECNO

The EMPRETECNO initiative was implemented to support the creation of technology-based firms in a variety of sectors. The program was designed to fulfill three objectives: (a) contribute to the creation of new technology-based businesses by helping them to attract additional private investments, (b) stimulate the flow of ideas from the national innovation system and translate them into economic activity and growth outcomes, and (c) foster stronger public-private partnerships. Program beneficiaries included individuals with a proven ability to develop scientific research or innovation, private firms, universities, and other public institutions within the national innovation system.

EMPRETECNO launched three calls for proposals in 2009, 2016, and 2017 to support entrepreneurs in building viable, knowledge-based business. Of the 304 projects submitted, 126 were selected to receive financial and related technical support. The program provided a nonreimbursable matching grant of up to

75 percent of the total project cost (or a maximum amount of US$2.5 million per project), with at least the remaining 25 percent of the project cost financed by the beneficiaries.

Projects supported under the first of these calls have now been fully financed and completed. In this chapter, we present the results of an impact evaluation using quasi-experimental evaluation design with a difference-in-difference (DD) model combined with propensity score matching (PSM) to estimate the program's impact on the likelihood of business creation, rate of new business survival, and likelihood of crowding in private financing. The two more recent calls, which are still under way, have also achieved interesting results, but could not be included in the impact evaluation due to their ongoing nature. In this chapter, we provide the results of the impact evaluation of the first call of EMPRETECNO, followed by insights from field interviews with a sample of beneficiaries from all three calls.

Impact evaluation of EMPRETECNO PAEBT

Treatment group

The treatment group in this evaluation included teams of entrepreneurs who obtained support from EMPRETECNO PAEBT (EMPRETECNO's first call for proposals). On average, these projects were started and finalized between 2013 and 2016, allowing us to study the impact of the program two years following the intervention.

Control group

The control group consisted of teams who had requested but not received a subsidy from the program.

Outcome variables

The impact evaluation considered three outcome variables: (a) rate of creation of a new technology-based firm, (b) age of the firm, and (c) rate of success raising private capital.

Methodology

The database for the evaluation combined two sources of information: (a) the administrative records of FONARSEC, including both applicants and program beneficiaries; and (b) an existing database that contains information on EMPRETECNO applicants from before and after the program. These data were used to construct panel data including 209 entrepreneur teams and 418 observations.

Results

The impact evaluation shows that being a beneficiary of the program has a significant correlation with increased creation of technology-based firms and ability to obtain private capital (table 4.1). In addition, longer-lived firms have an increased ability to obtain private capital.

Field interviews and qualitative analysis

The evaluation of EMPRETECNO's first round was complemented with field visits to 35 recent beneficiaries. According to these field visits, the program's success

TABLE 4.1 **Estimated effect of EMPRETECNO PAEBT**

INDICATOR	TECHNOLOGY-BASED FIRM CREATED	OBTAIN PRIVATE CAPITAL	AGE OF THE FIRM (MONTHS)
Beneficiary of PAEBT	0.296*** (0.068)	0.128** (0.050)	15.590*** (3.424)
PhD	−0.195 (0.204)	0.038 (0.154)	4.769 (9.806)
CONICET	−0.049 (0.094)	−0.059 (0.071)	−0.147 (4.498)
Budget	0.000 (0.000)	0.000 (0.000)	−0.000 (0.000)
Constant	−0.256 (0.343)	−0.154 (0.258)	6.382 (16.469)
Observations	367	367	367
Entrepreneur teams	188	188	188
R-squared	0.615	0.168	0.808
Year dummy	YES	YES	YES

Source: World Bank.
Note: Estimated results of the first two columns correspond to a linar probability model with fixed effects. Robust standard errors are in parentheses. CONICET = National Scientific and Technical Research Council.
$^{**}p<.05$ $^{***}p<.01$

rate was also high in subsequent stages, with 75 percent early survival rates for firms: in the United States, 60 percent of all venture-backed start-ups fail (Ghosh 2012). The program received more than 200 submissions and supported 102 of these applicants with technical assistance and seed financing; of these applicants, as of early 2019, 76 became registered new businesses, with positive revenues; most of these firms broke even within the first two years of operations.

Beneficiaries also showed strong growth rates, with more than half becoming exporters within a few years. On average, businesses reached US$80,000–US$100,000 annually in revenues in their first one to three years. This suggests a potential to generate more than US$6 million annually within the median band of beneficiaries, assuming a consistent growth rate in sales. Also worth noting are the outliers ("money makers" in venture capital terms), which are expected to generate sales ranging between US$10 million and US$30 million annually, with strong export potential. Based on these sales estimates, the program's economic rate of return was 45 percent. These figures are especially impressive in comparison with the rest of the Argentine economy, which experienced a net decrease in annual sales in all sectors, according to the World Bank 2017 Enterprise Survey (figure 4.1).

Discussions with beneficiaries and a preliminary review of the ongoing evaluations highlight several elements of the program's design and implementation as contributing to the results. Most important, the availability of financing played an important role across beneficiaries, with all interviewees citing that they had explored other sources of seed financing and failed to find any in Argentina or elsewhere prior to the initiative. Entrepreneurs listed challenges related to (a) the high cost of finance and the shallowness of Argentine capital markets, (b) the inability of financial markets to assess and respond to the risk profiles of early-stage innovative ventures, (c) lack of collateral, and (d) limited management capabilities. The program invested an average of US$80,000–US$160,000 per new firm, primarily seed capital for most beneficiaries. Many of these

FIGURE 4.1
Change in real annual sales in Argentina, by sector, 2017

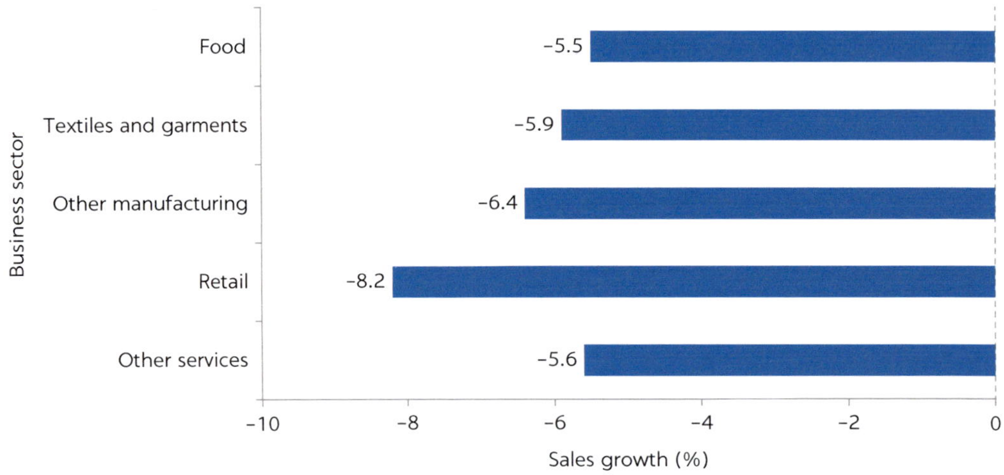

Source: World Bank 2017.

beneficiaries were then able to leverage additional financing from banks or private equity at later stages, once they had completed lab-stage product validation (at a minimum). Other factors contributed to the success of these entrepreneurs, including (a) the development of management capabilities, including support for business plan development; (b) follow-through and mentoring; and (c) efforts to address information asymmetries with public research agencies and build commercially valuable connections.

PUBLIC-PRIVATE PARTNERSHIPS: FONARSEC

FONARSEC was created in January 2009 to develop critical capacities within the productive sectors in areas of high potential impact. FONARSEC focused on reorienting public research capacities toward productive partnerships with the private sector using investments in research consortiums. It financed the creation of new capacities and the development of platforms in general-purpose technologies or multipurpose technologies (biotechnology, nanotechnology, and information and communication technology [ICT]) through support for large innovation projects with a clear economic and social impact. During its first 10 years of existence, FONARSEC focused on the three fundamental objectives that fostered its creation: the association, focalization, and organization of the public-private sector.

The initiative created a total of 29 associative consortiums (public-private and private-private) across different fields, which resulted in new products and added value in their respective industries. The program invested an average of US$1.2 million in each partnership, with two-thirds of the financing allocated to public institutions and the remaining third directed to the private sector. The acquisition of capital goods and infrastructure spending accounted for 64 percent and 13 percent of the budgets, respectively. A wide range of applications and derivations of the original research ideas resulted in new products and services that were previously not possible or contemplated. Some examples of such product lines or services include (a) new drought-tolerant alfalfa breeds (with significant implications for agricultural productivity); (b) a vaccine for aphthous fever; (c) a unified, computerized, remote-access database for knowledge sharing; (d) new products in light manufacturing, such as an antiparasitic for pets, anticellulite socks, flame-retardant textiles, and so forth; and (e) new products that improve heavy manufacturing competitiveness, such as a GPRS antenna for E-trac and E-BUS systems, an electric inverter–type welding machine, a wireless network for industrial monitoring based on energy-harvesting techniques, and an assistance system for preventive maintenance in industrial plants.

Impact evaluation

Treatment group

This evaluation included 18 public-private associative consortiums encompassing 50 private companies and 30 public stakeholders. The projects financed were linked to technological platforms such as agro-biotechnology, biotechnology, nanotechnology, and ICT. According to the administrative registers from FONARSEC, these projects began—on average—during 2012 and ended between 2015 and 2016. At the time of the evaluation, at least two years had passed since the finalization of each project, a window that allowed us to analyze the effect attributable to the FSATs. The treatment group includes private firms that belong to the beneficiary consortiums.

Control group

The ANR TEC (Nonreimbursable Grants for Technology Projects [Aportes No Reembolsables Technología]) Program[1] financed projects oriented toward biotechnology, nanotechnology, and ICTs during the same period of time as the FSAT. The main difference between the two programs pertains to the type of beneficiary and the amount of public support: FSAT beneficiaries were public-private consortiums, while ANR TEC beneficiaries were firms. To improve comparability, we included a set of variables that indicate the firms' expertise and ability to formulate good projects and obtain public financing.

Data and main variables

To build the database, we merged the list of firms that integrate both treatment and comparison groups with the innovation survey of the Argentine Technological Fund (FONTAR). The integration yielded a balanced panel of data for 111 firms with 222 observations. Among them, 34 firms correspond to the treatment group, and the remaining 77 correspond to the control group. These panel data include information at two points in time: before and after the program. Table 4.2 describes the main variables used.

Methodology

As before, we use a difference-in-difference model combined with propensity score matching. DD models compare changes over time between a group unaffected by the policy with a group affected by the public intervention; they attribute the "difference-in-differences" to the effect of the policy. DD methods provide unbiased effect estimates if the trend over time would have been the same between the treatment and comparison groups in the absence of the intervention. However, a concern with DD models is that the program and intervention groups may differ in ways that are related to their trends over

TABLE 4.2 **Description of the main variables used in the evaluation**

VARIABLE	DESCRIPTION	VALUES
Employment	Firms' total employment	Thousands of US dollars per year
Sales	Firms' total sales	Thousands of US dollars per year
Exports	Firms' exports	Thousands of US dollars per year
Exporting	Exporting activity of the firm	1 if firms' exports are greater than zero, 0 otherwise
R&D intensity	Ratio of R&D expenditures to firms' total employment	Thousands of US dollars per employee
Innovation activities intensity	Ratio of innovation expenditures to firms' total employment	Thousands of US dollars per employee
AMBA	Geographic location of firms	1 if the firm is located in the city or the province of Buenos Aires, 0 otherwise
FONTAR presentations (before FSAT)	Number of times the firm requested public support from FONTAR	0 to …
FONTAR adjudications (before FSAT)	Number of times the firm received a public support from FONTAR	0 to …
Sector	Set of binary variables that indicates sectorial fixed effects	ISIC rev 3.1

Source: World Bank.
Note: AMBA = available in metropolitan Buenos Aires; FSAT = sectoral funds; FONTAR = Argentine Technological Fund; R&D = research and development.

time or that their compositions may change over time. Although this assumption cannot be tested, a widely accepted practice for strengthening the credibility of the DD model is to show that these trends were equal before the period analyzed. Along this line, PSM can be used to identify a comparison group that was similar to the treatment group in all of the relevant pretreatment variables and pretreatment trends of the outcome variable.

Results

Estimated results confirm that, for beneficiary firms, having participated in the FSAT positively affected their effort in innovation activities (table 4.3). Specifically, innovation intensity per employee grew at a more intense rate than would have been registered in the absence of a program. We also estimated the effect of the program on the firm's performance. We focused on the trajectory of employment, sales, and sales per employee. On the one hand, the results confirm that having participated in any of the beneficiary consortiums led to greater growth, both in employment and in sales. In other words, if the firms had not participated in the program, they would have shown a trajectory with less accentuated growth. On the other hand, we cannot confirm that the program affected firms' productivity. However, this result must be treated with caution due to the short time that had passed since the end of the program. The evidence shows that public innovation programs affect firms' productivity starting in the sixth year (Fiorentin, Pereira, and Suárez 2018).

TABLE 4.3 **Estimated effect of the FSAT program**

INDICATOR	EMPLOYMENT (LOG)	SALES (LOG)	SALES PER EMPLOYEE (LOG)
FSAT	0.134** (0.017)	0.094*** (0.041)	−0.134 (0.124)
AI per employee (log)	−0.037 (0.069)	0.137 (0.097)	0.239*** (0.085)
I+D per employee (log)	−0.005 (0.044)	0.007 (0.054)	−0.019 (0.045)
Exports	0.000 (0.000)	−0.000 (0.000)	0.000 (0.000)
= 1 if exports	0.011 (0.206)	0.253 (0.254)	0.218 (0.212)
Sales	0.000 (0.000)		0.000*** (0.000)
Employment		0.004 (0.003)	−0.014*** (0.003)
Employment^2		−0.000 (0.000)	0.000** (0.000)
Constant	3.870*** (0.524)	7.103*** (1.117)	1.120 (0.966)
Observations	175	178	175
Number of firms	100	100	100
R-squared	0.309	0.715	0.812
Year dummy	YES	YES	YES

Source: World Bank.
Note: FSAT = sectoral funds.
***p<.01 ***p<.05*

Field interviews and qualitative analysis of FSAT

FSAT partnerships had a demonstrated effect and continue to show signs of sustainability. To date, 60 percent of the reporting public institutions indicated a change in their research and development trajectory as a result of the initiative. As of 2019, one in four consortiums remained operational, although the related projects have been formally concluded. In some cases, firms have expressed an interest in pursuing private financing for projects developed under the program, resulting in the creation of new companies. Many of these partnerships have demonstrated the ability to take better advantage of assets in research and human capital by building bridges between the private and public sectors and creating and sharing commercial and social objectives. Many of the interventions supported were able to obtain private sector support that had previously not been accessible for isolated and uncommercialized research.

Other noteworthy results include the following:

- *Ability to catalyze or crowd in additional investment.* Many of the supported consortiums resulted in the creation of new companies or product lines that were able to crowd in very significant additional investments in subsequent stages. For example, six public-private partnerships for which data are available were able to obtain more than US$60 million in additional investments because they used the seed financing to demonstrate product viability (for less than US$8 million invested in total across all). These firms also entered into additional agreements and are expected to raise another US$42 million from private investors in the next two years.

- *Spillovers into productivity and value addition within the broader sectors of beneficiaries are promising.* For example, a public-private partnership developed eight new alfalfa breeds, based on a publicly financed technology initiated by the National Science and Technical Research Council (CONICET), and produced a commercial application for the first time. These products significantly enhance the drought and salinity tolerance of alfalfa and increase yields 20 percent to 30 percent in dairy and cattle industries in the trials to date. These plants are viable for 40 percent of dairy and beef production in Argentina and stand to improve significantly and at large scale the drought tolerance and overall productivity of the industry. Since then, some of the technologies have received patents in Argentina, Australia, Paraguay, and the United States and many more patents have been filed around the world.
- *Import substitution and reduction in public spending.* Several public-private partnerships reduced public spending in critical areas such as health. For example, one of the consortiums produced two biosimilar cancer drugs that reduced the price of equivalent drugs on the market between 53 percent and 62 percent. The partnership subsequently captured 70–75 percent of the market in Argentina alone, resulting in US$91 million in annual currency savings and more than US$300 million in total savings to the health system.

The field visits and a preliminary review of the ongoing evaluations found that some elements of the program's design and implementation may have contributed to these results:

- The initiative focused on information asymmetries and coordination failures between the private sector and public research by introducing incentives for partnerships through a results-oriented financing scheme and by developing the broader institutional capacity for improved coordination.
- The project financing helped to address the initial transaction costs of the partnership, which was critical given that such partnerships are rare and their risks and feasibility are unknown. The financing also served as seed financing that covered the one-time costs of equipment needed to transform the original research into a commercial product. Such support is especially important given the limited access to finance in Argentina.

The project allowed for partnerships to be developed based on both commercially viable outcomes and overall economic and social impact objectives (such as drought-tolerant alfalfa that stands to have a significant impact on the dairy and beef industries or new tools that increase the ability to introduce early diagnosis of disease and cut costs in public health spending).

NOTE

1. A program of the Argentine Technological Fund, which finances partially bioengineering projects, nanotechnology, and ICTs and seeks to increase development and innovation capacities and to create and strengthen technological platforms.

REFERENCES

Fiorentin, Florencia Alejandra, Mariano Pereira, and Diana Valeria Suárez. 2018. "As Times Goes By: A Dynamic Impact Assessment of the Innovation Policy and the Matthew Effect on Argentinean Firms." *Economics of Innovation and New Technology* 28 (7): 657–73.

Ghosh, Shikar. 2012. "The Venture Capital Secret: 3 Out of 4 Start-Ups Fail." Harvard Business School, Cambridge, MA.

IAMC (Instituto Argentino del Mercado de Capitales). 1999. "Políticas para las pequeñas y medianas empresas: Evaluación y propuestas." IAMC, Buenos Aires.

McDermott, Gerald. 2000. "Argentine SMEs and Their Support Programs: The Barriers and Possibilities for Local Learning." Wharton School of Business, University of Pennsylvania, Philadelphia.

World Bank. 2017. World Bank Enterprise Survey (database). Washington, DC: World Bank.

5 Conclusions and Recommendations

Argentina is widely admired for comparative strengths in its natural capital and, in particular, its human capital and research excellence—strengths upon which it can build with smart policies and targeted investments. Traditionally, the Argentine science, technology, and innovation (STI) system has been driven by supply and overly focused on science and research; in recent years, however, government policies have been focusing more on the linkages with the private sector and production. This trend needs to continue and intensify. There is still a disconnect between Argentina's growth demands, private sector, and the research output as well as a misalignment between national priorities and resource allocation. Although scientific production in Argentina is relatively strong compared to that of its peers, technology transfer and adoption by firms remain low.

To improve these outcomes, Argentina needs to approach innovation policy more holistically, focus on gaps in the innovation function and firm-level capabilities, and ultimately tailor policies more closely to market failures. In the past two decades, Argentina has been working to reduce the shortage of human capital and institutions specialized in technology transfer, to bridge the gaps between both sides, and to address the lack of incentives to engage. Early signs from these efforts suggest that they can indeed yield results, and they should be scaled up where possible to crowd in additional financing from the private sector.

However, recent trends in fiscal consolidation risk reversing progress made in aligning the STI policy mix with Argentina's agenda for growth and diversification. Given the limited resources available, maximizing the effectiveness of the resources allocated to promoting innovation is more important than ever. This effort includes ensuring high-quality monitoring and evaluation of results and the underlying data, enhanced coordination between the various line agencies involved, and better identification of strengths, assets, and bottlenecks, along with the ability to scale up or correct course when needed based on ongoing data and results. Argentina's recent fiscal consolidation and realignment and budget reductions within the STI policy mix could undermine the government's overall goals of increasing productive innovation and diversification. The fiscal consolidation process of 2017–18 disproportionately affected STI policies, which risks undermining the key microeconomic foundations of long-term growth.

Against this backdrop, five areas emerge as priorities for policy intervention.

First, develop a medium- to long-term, fiscally responsible innovation strategy to enhance institutional stability and policy consistency and maximize the contributions to growth. Using a holistic approach, Argentina should align innovation policy more closely with sustainable growth objectives and develop a medium-term strategy to generate a shared vision and a stable institutional environment over the long run. Institutional stability and policy predictability are critical to enabling innovation policies to achieve their objectives. Without long-term countercyclical investment, policy reversals are likely to emerge as a result of fiscal consolidation pressures.

Second, align public spending on innovation more closely with national priorities. Programs focusing on exports, diversification, and entrepreneurship were hit the hardest during the recent fiscal consolidation. Following better monitoring and evaluation (M&E) systems and improved data, STI policies should evaluate the economic rate of return of innovation investments in terms of the following:

- *Contribution to sustained growth and shared prosperity:* Improved private sector competitiveness and performance in terms of sales growth, firm and job creation, and impact on per capita income growth
- *Diversification and current account impact:* Increase in net exports and sources of economic growth
- *Productivity at-large:* Existence of productivity spillovers across both traditional and emerging sectors
- *Fiscal prudence:* Ability to create savings and enable efficiencies in public spending and prioritize, scale up, and correct course accordingly.

Third, maximize the impact of the existing assets in science and research inputs by focusing on complementary policies such as firm-level capabilities and by promoting academic entrepreneurship and public-private partnerships. Recent programs in the Argentine Technological Fund (FONTAR) and Argentine Sectoral Fund (FONARSEC) provide a precedent on how to crowd in private financing using better alignment of incentives, strategic financial support to subsidize transaction costs, professional and accountable governance structures, and results-oriented market-led partnership designs. Facilitating patent registration and other intellectual property systems is also key; however, legal capabilities within the public institutions charged with registering patents were significantly downsized recently.

Fourth, develop flexible STI policies that adapt to the needs of local innovation systems, building on national knowledge assets and institutions. Innovation policies should improve regional public sector capabilities to facilitate coordination with national programs and technology adoption. Additionally, policy should capitalize on existing regional assets and build on large institutional systems like the National Science and Technical Research Council (CONICET).

Fifth, mainstream evidence-based policy making to recalibrate and realign STI policies periodically with the country's agenda for growth and productive diversification. Design policy instruments in response to specific market failures at different stages of the innovation cycle, including the following:

- *Focus on supporting firm- and entrepreneur-level productivity and innovation in periods of economic uncertainty.* For example, the emphasis on tax incentives is inconsistent with pro-market or pro-competition principles; as such, tax incentives are not an effective instrument for addressing market failures that affect innovation performance. Incumbents automatically benefit from tax incentives, while new entrants and early-stage innovators do not. Even more important, tax incentives do little to support absorptive capacity.

- *Focus on innovation and absorptive capacity with programs designed to support management capabilities.* Current STI policies focus on incremental improvements in existing production capacity—such as acquisition of machinery and improvement of managerial capacity and non–research and development activities. While these policies appear to improve absorptive capacity, building firm-level innovative capacity is not limited to what can simply be bought in the market. It is essential to build new knowledge and capacity within firms, such as obtaining certifications and developing complex linkages with other actors.
- *Increase support for young and new innovative ventures.* The current mix of STI in Argentina targets mature firms in traditional sectors; new and more innovative ventures are needed to improve the quality of the growth process.
- *Realign STI policies toward firm-level support to improve Argentina's stronger integration with global markets.* Recent budget reductions for export promotion and support for obtaining international certifications are inconsistent with an export competitiveness strategy.
- *Improve data systems and M&E functions.* M&E systems help to improve the efficiency and impact of policy. Argentina needs to develop and sustain requisite data sets and M&E systems to monitor innovation inputs, outputs, results, and expected impact. Impact evaluations should also be incorporated in program design and implementation (including course correction, targeting, and experimentation).
- *Increase transparency and data accessibility, a critical building block of evidence-based STI policies.* Access to STI data remains fragmented and ad hoc. Providing the public with online access to information on the STI policy mix would support evaluation and crowdsourcing for ideas and experimentation.

APPENDIX A

Regional Heterogeneity and Innovation

Regional heterogeneity of economic activity is pronounced in Argentina. While the distribution of businesses by size is similar across provinces, other differences are stark, including income, industrial mix, and population density. As shown in figure A.1, the distribution of micro, small, and medium enterprises is similar across the provinces of Jujuy, Neuquén, Salta, and Santa Fe. Gross domestic product (GDP) per capita, however, ranges from US$7,807 (Salta) to more than US$31,000 (Neuquén). The industrial mix of each province also varies considerably, with hydrocarbons most prevalent in Neuquén and agroindustrials most prevalent in Santa Fe. While Neuquén has the lowest population density, it has the highest GDP per capita of these four provinces, demonstrating that simple urban-rural explanations do not explain the variations in income. Research and development (R&D) spending is concentrated in Buenos Aires Province (33.9 percent), the City of Buenos Aires (26.8 percent), Córdoba (8.1 percent), and Santa Fe (5 percent).

From the perspective of innovation, these regional differences call for tailored policies to facilitate more effective knowledge diffusion and technology transfer within the country. Argentina has a strong network of research institutes and R&D capacity, but this asset needs to translate appropriately across

FIGURE A.1

Number of businesses in four provinces of Argentina, by firm size, 2015

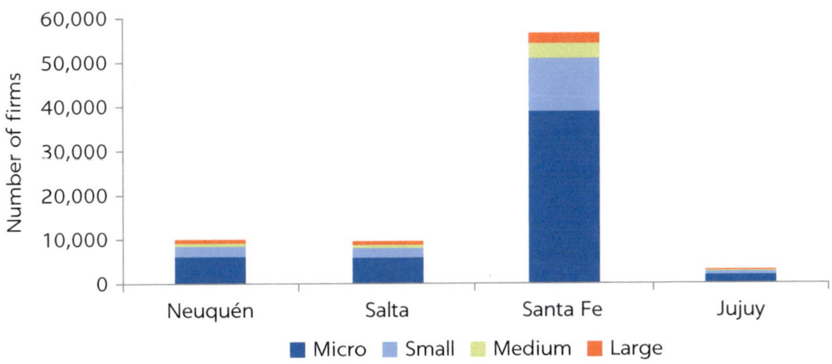

Source: National Institute of Statistics and Censuses, Argentina.

all regions. For example, the tourism sector in Jujuy has led the way in digital innovation, whereas mining is the primary industry in Neuquén. Moreover, insufficient public sector and private sector capabilities, along with the absence of linkages between the supply of and demand for knowledge and technology solutions, can explain some of the disparities in productive capacity, technology adoption, and knowledge diffusion across the regions. Federal innovation programs are subject to a self-selection bias, which leads to a greater concentration of beneficiaries within regions that have higher capacity in these areas. For example, the Agencia Nacional de Promoción Cientifica y Tecnológica (Agencia I+D+I) has most of its beneficiaries in the city and province of Buenos Aires, Córdoba, and Santa Fe. National Science and Technical Research Council (CONICET) laboratories, research groups, and publications are concentrated mainly in the city of Buenos Aires and in the hub in Santa Fe and Rosario. However, well-known CONICET centers and innovation hubs are also located in other regions, such as Chubut, anchored in natural resources, and Neuquén, which has a history of frontier research in the nuclear and space programs. These centers provide examples of regional innovation policies.

Regions with insufficient public sector capabilities suffer from limited publicly funded research and limited capacity for development of new research projects or bridging to projects at the federal level. As such, research output is concentrated in larger innovation hubs—for example, CONICET projects are concentrated in the province and city of Buenos Aires, Córdoba, and Santa Fe. CONICET-funded PhD researchers are also overrepresented in these hubs. Moreover, achieving technology adoption and transfer requires other actors such as accelerators, technology transfer units in universities and in the private sector, public-private infrastructure and other collaboration facilities, and public sector institutions such as regional innovation agencies and ministries. Support to develop a network of such actors plays an important role in fostering regional innovation. Actors that facilitate linkages for technology transfer are particularly lacking outside of the current innovation hubs.

This appendix elaborates on the differences in economic characteristics across provinces by focusing on four sample provinces.

REGIONAL ECONOMIC DIFFERENCES ILLUSTRATED: NEUQUÉN, SALTA, SANTA FE, AND JUJUY

Neuquén Province

Neuquén Province has a population of 628,897, representing 1.4 percent of Argentina's total population. Population density is 6.7 persons per square kilometer, far above the 1.4 persons per square kilometer average for the Patagonia region. The province accounts for 30.9 percent of Patagonian GDP and 3.1 percent of national GDP. GDP per capita, at US$31,429, is much higher than at the national level (US$14,402). GDP is split almost evenly between goods (49.4 percent) and services (50.6 percent). The mining sector represents 33.2 percent of the economy, with hydrocarbons constituting the majority of this sector. Neuquén Province produces most of the country's gas and a large amount of its natural gas.

In all, 9,933 companies are registered in Neuquén, 1.6 percent of the national total. Of these, 81.4 percent operate in the services sector. The distribution of micro, small, medium, and large enterprises is detailed in figure A.2. Between 2013 to 2016, the different sectors grew in terms of the number of companies, as shown in figure A.3.

The services sector accounts for 60.3 percent of registered employment, with goods comprising the remaining 39.7 percent. Figure A.4 shows the number of employees per sector.

Private sector salaries average Arg$39,475 per year, more than 50 percent higher than the national average. The mining sector is the highest paid, at an average salary of more than Arg$80,000.

Neuquén's exports represent 0.1 percent of national exports (figure A.5). In recent years, Neuquén's exports have fallen, primarily due to the fall in fuel and energy exports.

FIGURE A.2

Distribution of businesses in Neuquén Province, by firm size

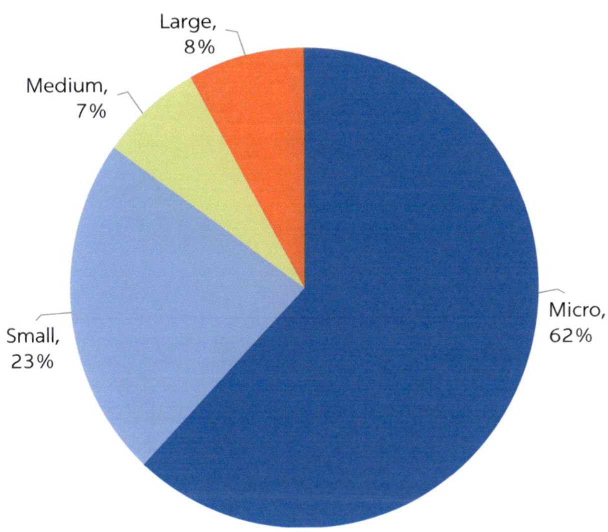

Source: Ministry of Production, Argentina.

FIGURE A.3

Change in number of businesses in Neuquén Province, by sector, 2013–16

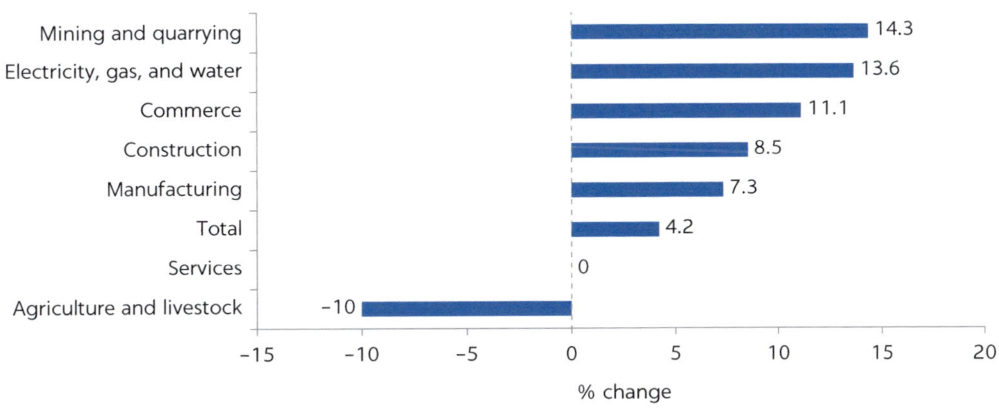

Source: Employment and Business Dynamics Observatory, Ministry of Production, Argentina.

FIGURE A.4

Number of employees in Neuquén Province, by sector, 2017

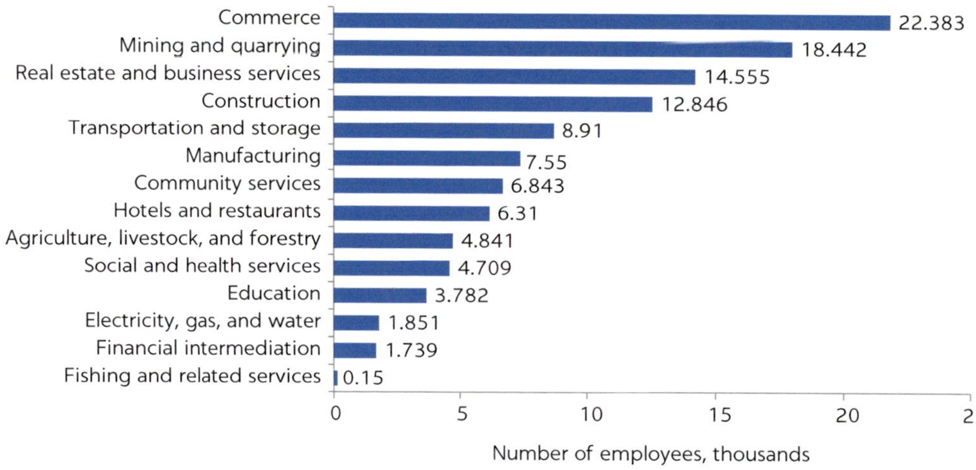

Source: Employment and Business Dynamics Observatory, Ministry of Production, Argentina (2017 data).

FIGURE A.5

Value of exports from Neuquén Province, 2010–17

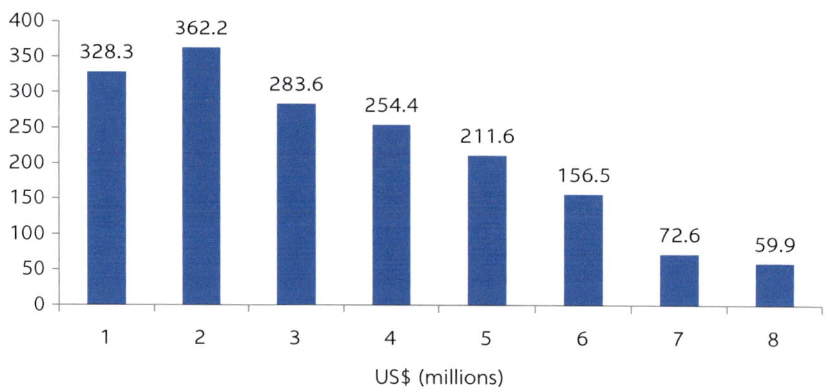

Source: National Institute of Statistics and Censuses, Argentina.

Salta Province

Salta Province has a population of 1,388,532, representing 3.1 percent of Argentina's total population. The population density is 8.9 persons per square kilometer, below that of the 11.8 and 11.9 persons per square kilometer average for the Northeast region and the national level, respectively. Salta Province accounts for 25.2 percent of GDP for the Northwest region and 1.7 percent of national GDP. GDP per capita, at US$7,807, is much lower than the national level (US$14,402).

GDP is slightly skewed toward services, at 56.9 percent. Trade accounts for 15.5 percent of GDP, followed by real estate and business services (9.2 percent). Public administration and education together account for 14.1 percent of GDP. Among the various goods sectors, manufacturing represents the largest portion, at 13.4 percent, followed closely by livestock and forestry (11.4 percent) and mining (5.0 percent).

In all, 9,543 companies are registered in Salta, 1.8 percent of the national total. Of these, 71.8 percent operate in the services sector. The distribution of micro, small, medium, and large enterprises is detailed in figure A.6. Between 2013 to 2016, the number of companies grew overall, but declined in some sectors, as shown in figure A.7 in terms of the number of companies.

The services sector accounts for 57.2 percent of registered employment, with goods comprising the remaining 42.8 percent. Figure A.8 shows the number of employees per sector.

Private sector salaries average Arg$19,863 per year, about 24.3 percent below the national average. The mining sector is the highest paid, at Arg$49,675, closely followed by the electricity, gas, and water sector at Arg$45,090.

Salta's exports represent 1.6 percent of national exports. They have fallen in recent years, primarily due to the decline in fuel and energy exports (figure A.9).

FIGURE A.6

Distribution of businesses in Salta Province, by firm size

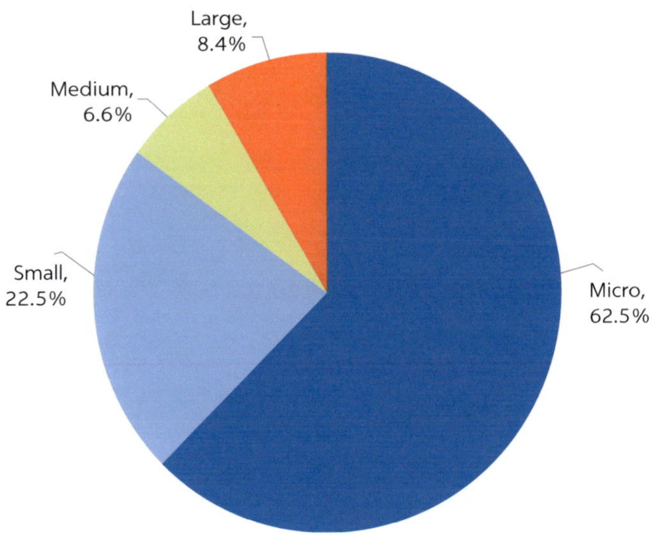

Source: Ministry of Production, Argentina.

FIGURE A.7

Change in the number of businesses in Salta Province, 2013–16

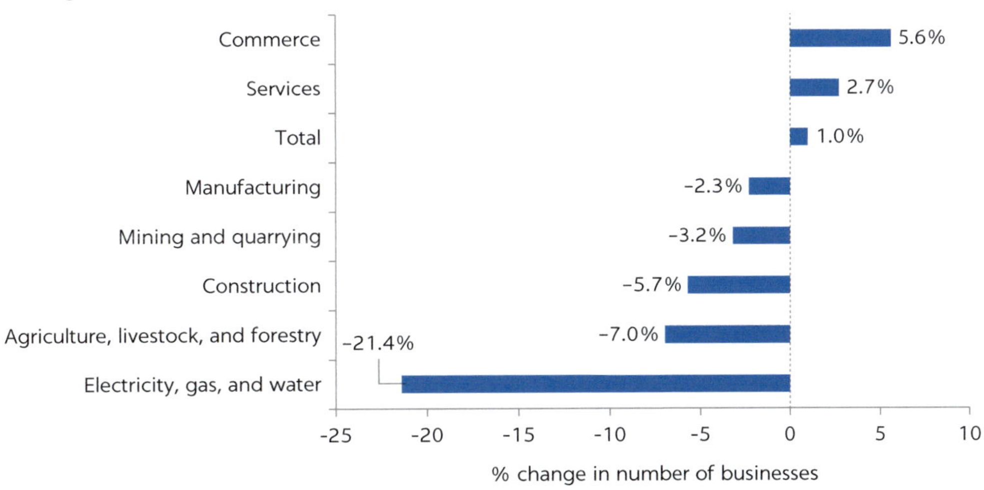

Source: Employment and Business Dynamics Observatory, Ministry of Production, Argentina.

FIGURE A.8
Number of employees in Salta Province, by sector, 2017

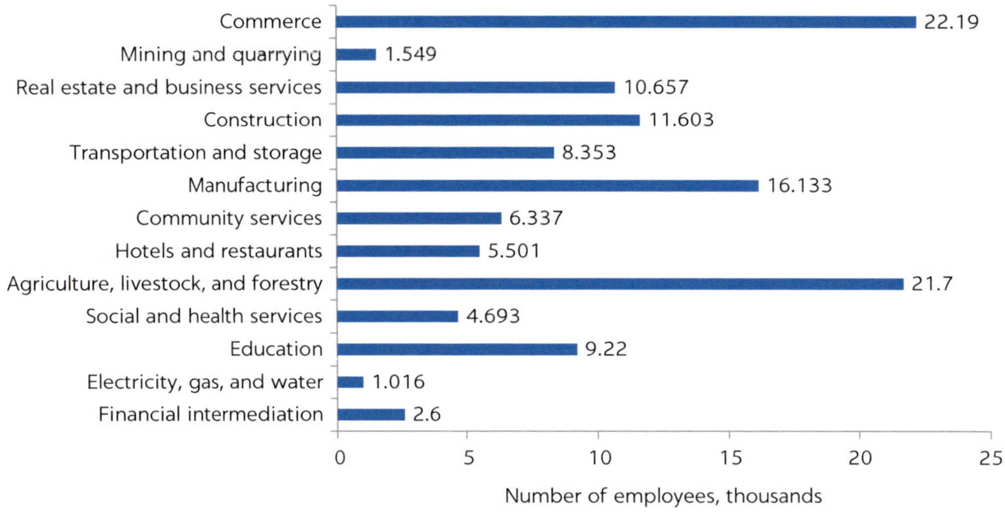

Source: Employment and Business Dynamics Observatory, Ministry of Production, Argentina (2017 data).

FIGURE A.9
Value of exports from Salta Province, 2012–17

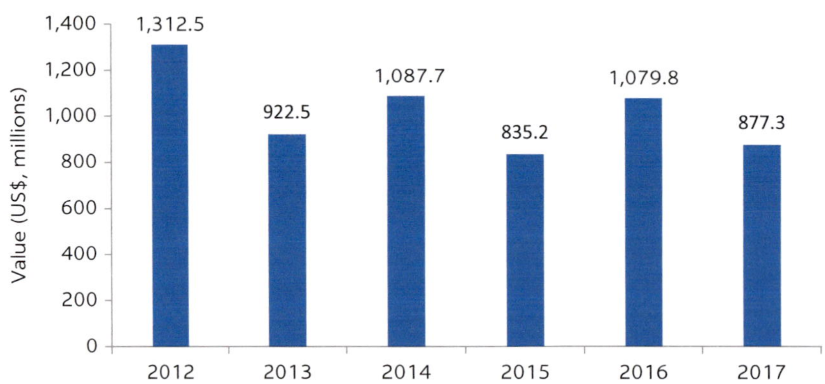

Source: National Institute of Statistics and Censuses, Argentina.

Santa Fe Province

Santa Fe Province has a population of 3,425,656, representing 7.9 percent of Argentina's total population. The population density is 25.8 persons per square kilometer, below that of the Central region and the city of Buenos Aires, at 42.3 persons per square kilometer. Santa Fe accounts for 9.2 percent of national GDP. GDP per capita is 11 percent higher than at the national level.

The primary economic activity takes place in the agroindustrial sector, including oil, meat, wheat, and dairy. The province also has well-established sectors outside of natural resources, including steel, machinery and equipment, chemical products, automotive products, and rubber and plastic products. Within the agriculture and livestock sectors, Santa Fe contributes 17.8 percent of the national production of soybeans, wheat crops, corn, and beef.

GDP is slightly skewed toward services, at 54 percent. Trade accounts for 22 percent of GDP, followed by (a) transportation, storage, and communications and (b) real estate and business services, at 8 percent. Among the various goods sectors, manufacturing represents the largest portion, at 27 percent, followed by agriculture, livestock, hunting, and forestry.

Santa Fe has the largest share of the electricity, gas, and water sector nationally, at 16.6 percent, followed closely by the commerce sector, at 14.6 percent, and the manufacturing and agriculture sectors, at 13.9 percent each.

Santa Fe also has 9,414 industrial establishments, with a large concentration in the town of Rosario and the city of Santa Fe. Most of these establishments produce food products.

In all, 57,143 companies are registered in Santa Fe, 9.5 percent of the national total. Of these, 52 percent of these companies operate in the services sector, followed by 34 percent in commerce and 14 percent in the industrial sector. The distribution of micro, small, medium, and large enterprises is detailed in figure A.10.

The distribution of these businesses by sector is shown in figure A.11, demonstrating the relative growth of the commerce sector.

Between 2006 and 2016, some sectors grew, while some declined, but the number of companies grew overall, as shown in figure A.12 in terms of the number of companies.

The services sector accounts for 49 percent of registered employment, with 22 percent in commerce and 29 percent in industry. Figure A.13 shows the number of employees per sector.

Private sector salaries average Arg$24,289 per year, about 7.4 percent below the national average. Salaries in air and maritime transport are the highest, at

FIGURE A.10

Distribution of businesses in Santa Fe Province, by firm size

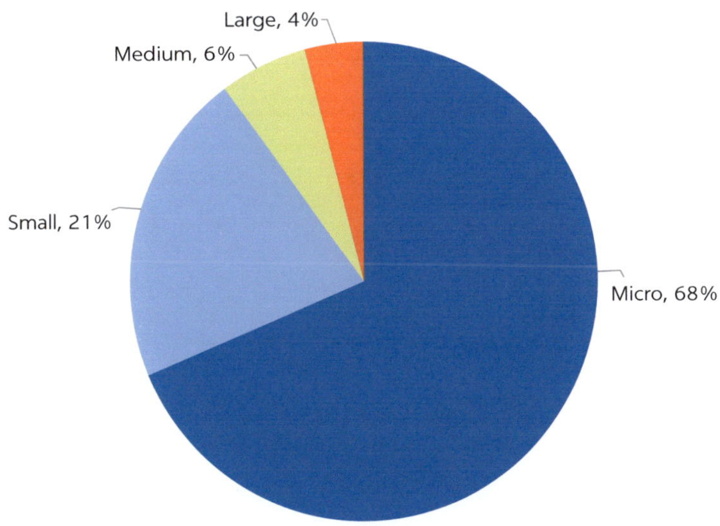

Source: Ministry of Production, Argentina.

FIGURE A.11

Distribution of businesses in Santa Fe Province, by sector, 2006 and 2016

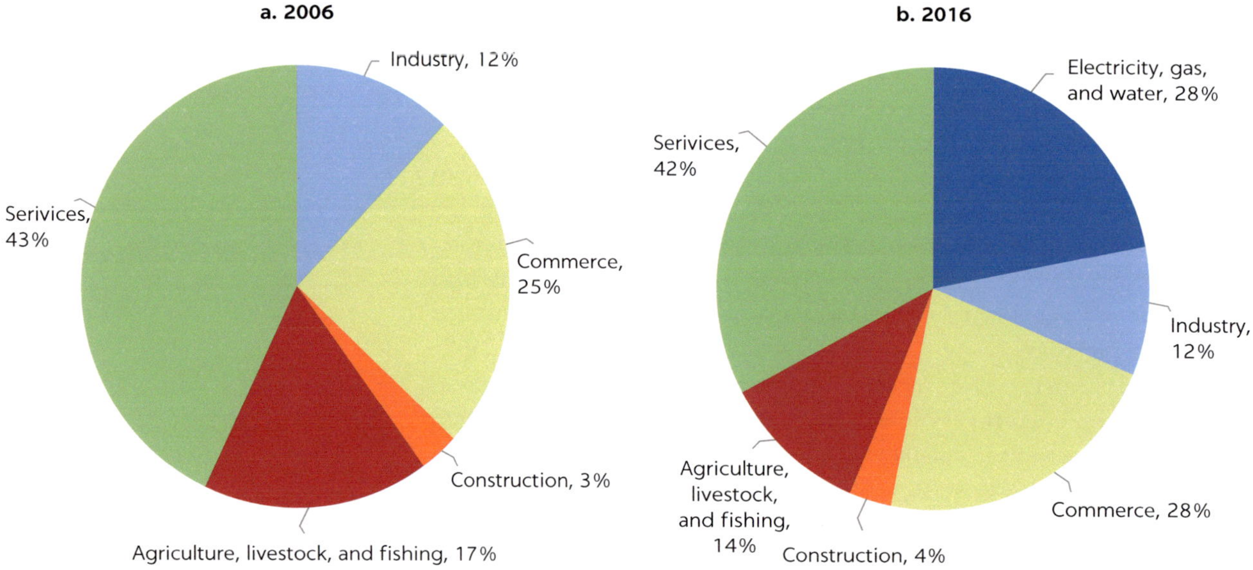

Source: Ministry of Production, Argentina.

FIGURE A.12

Change in the number of businesses in Santa Fe Province, by sector, 2006–16

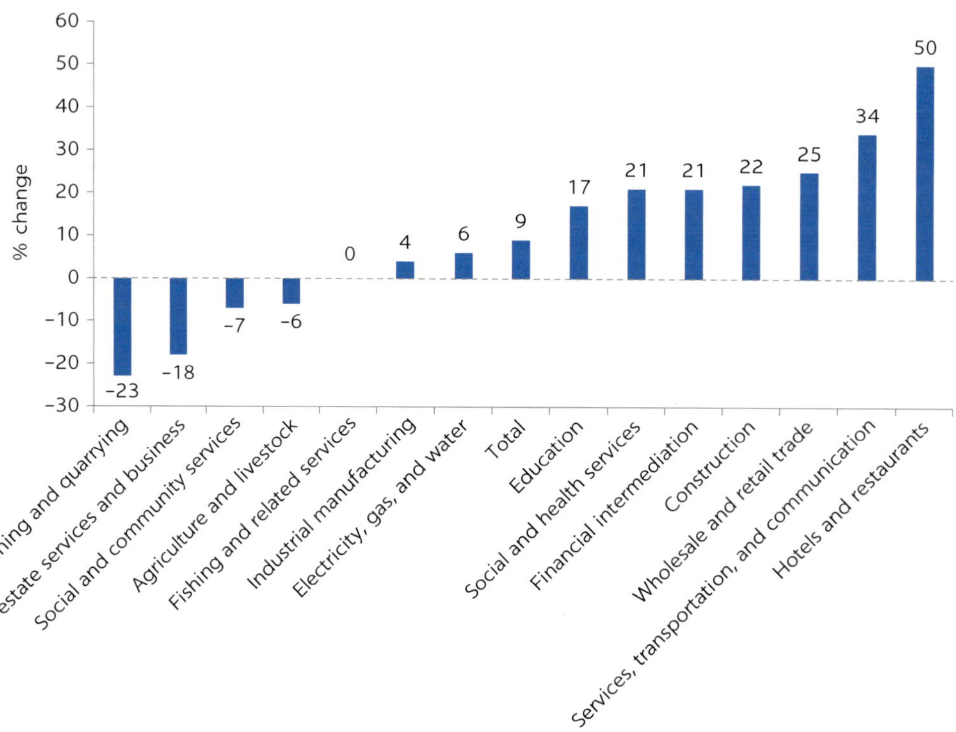

Source: Employment and Business Dynamics Observatory, Ministry of Production, Argentina.

FIGURE A.13
Number of employees in Santa Fe Province, by sector, 2017

Source: Employment and Business Dynamics Observatory, Ministry of Production, Argentina (2017 data).

TABLE A.1 **Santa Fe exports, 2017**

TOP 10 EXPORTS	US$	SHARE OF TOTAL (%)
Soy products	5,978,717,613	44.1
Soy oil	2,359,154,697	17.4
Biodiesel	943,738,251	7.0
Automobiles	584,414,861	4.3
Beef	401,783,793	3.0
Wheat	391,359,429	2.9
Soy	386,628,809	2.9
Corn	384,864,975	2.8
Leather	215,156,894	1.6
Automobile components	213,030,215	1.6

Source: National Institute of Statistics and Censuses, Argentina.

Arg$48,200, closely followed by the electricity, gas, and water sector, at Arg$47,196. The lowest average salary is in the hotel and restaurants sector. The average salary was Arg$29,788 in the industrial sector and Arg$16,972 in the agriculture, livestock, and fishing sector.

Santa Fe's exports represent 23.2 percent of national exports, second only to the city of Buenos Aires. The composition of Santa Fe's exports is shown in table A.1.

Jujuy Province

The distribution of businesses by firm size within the Jujuy Province is shown in figure A.14, followed by the number of businesses by sector in figure A.15.

FIGURE A.14
Distribution of businesses in Jujuy Province, by firm size

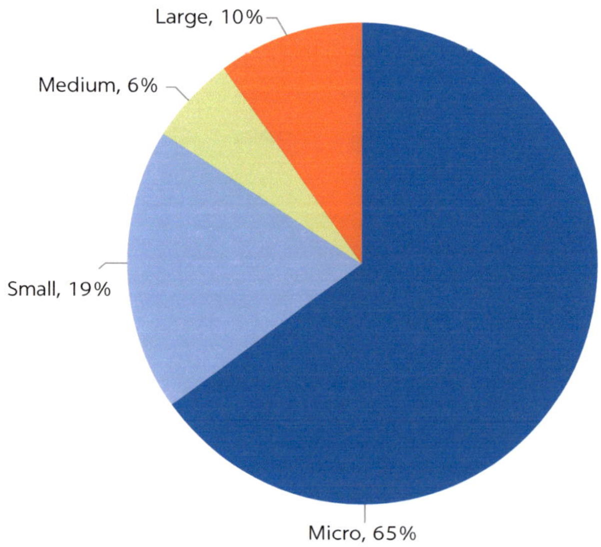

Source: Ministry of Production, Argentina.

FIGURE A.15
Number of businesses in Jujuy Province, by sector, 2016

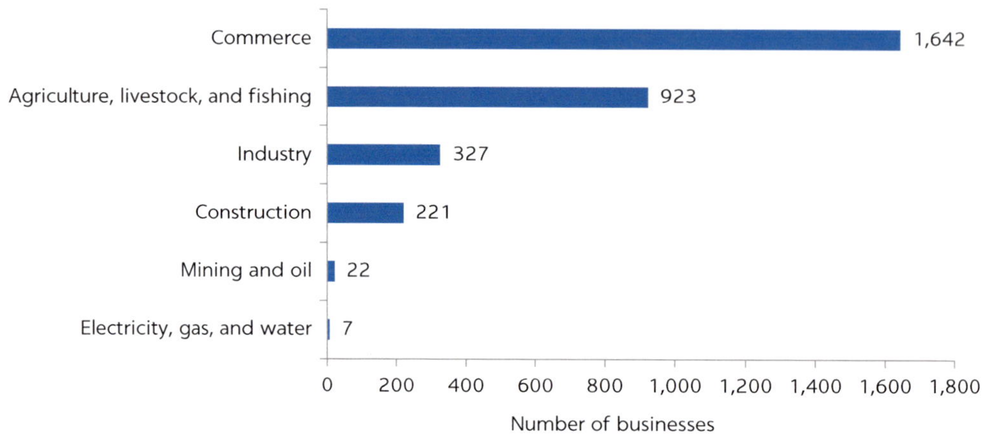

Source: Ministry of Production, Argentina.

The services sector accounts for 57.2 percent of registered employment, with goods comprising the remaining 42.8 percent. Figure A.16 shows the number of employees per sector.

Jujuy is the second fastest-growing province in Argentina. Exports have grown in relation to other provinces due to growth in the minerals, tourism, and agriculture sectors (figure A.17).

Traditional sectors such as tobacco and sugar production have started to incorporate new technologies and diversify production. Ledesma, the primary sugar producer, has now diversified into paper production, fruit juices, lemons, and oranges.

The tourism sector has been a tremendous provincial strength, as the center of the Southern Inca Empire. While tourism is not traditionally associated with innovation, the sector has increasingly driven the local

FIGURE A.16

Number of employees in Jujuy Province, by sector, 2017

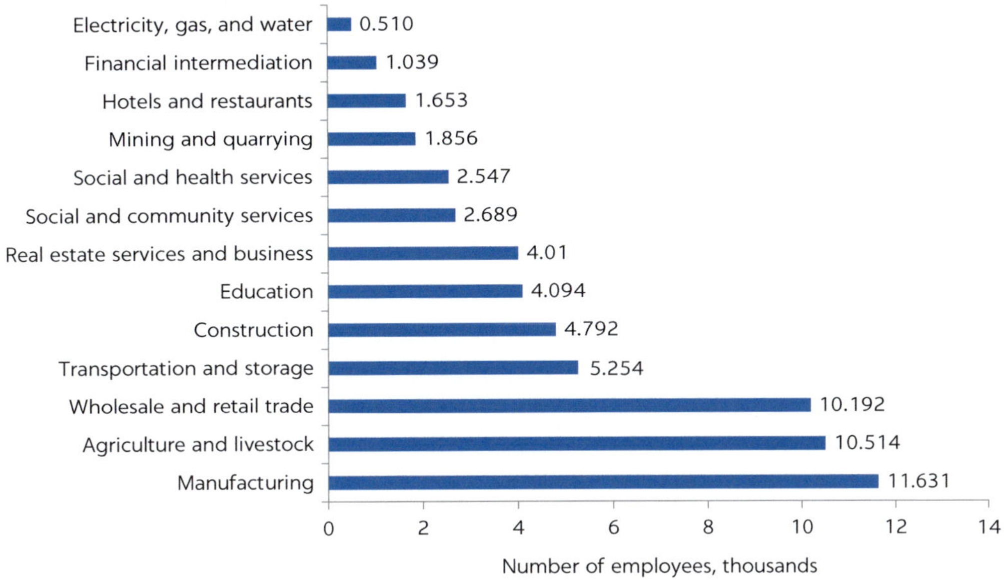

Source: Employment and Business Dynamics Observatory, Ministry of Production, Argentina (2017 data).

FIGURE A.17

Value of exports from Jujuy Province, 2012–17

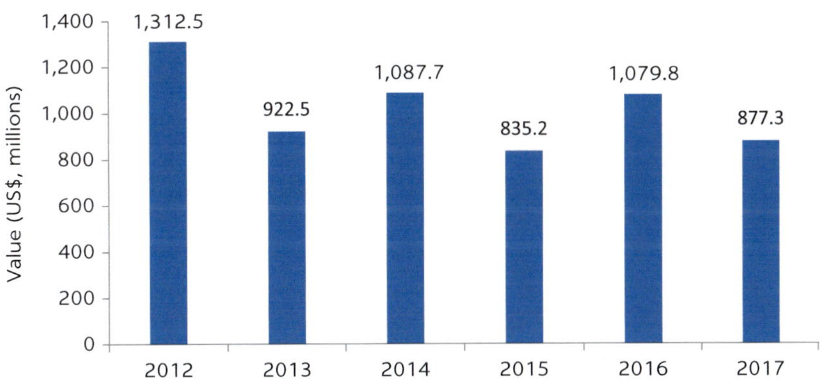

Source: National Institute of Statistics and Censuses, Argentina.

adoption of digital technologies and bottom-up innovation processes. Digital technologies build local capacity, networks, and assets, including villages and local communities.

Other sectors currently driving the demand for innovation within Jujuy include new-found lithium, along with copper and gold.

OVERVIEW OF FINDINGS AND POLICY IMPLICATIONS

Despite challenges, there are successful start-ups and technological adoption in Argentina's provinces. Our research identifies three types of provinces: frontier, emerging, and provinces with a tradition in science, technology, and innovation (STI) due to history, natural resources, or other specific factors. Frontier regions are characterized by a critical mass of many of the components of the national innovation system as well as by actors that link the national supply of knowledge with the regional and local demand for solutions. Emerging regions, in contrast, lack a significant number of actors and rely on idiosyncratic factors, such as the emergence of a local leader with personal networks, or the repatriation of success stories that incubate in the center and move back to the regions. Finally, there are some examples of specific success stories, such as the frontier research centers in Neuquén, dedicated to nuclear and satellite production, that are, however, disconnected from the regional economies.

Differentiated innovation policies can be tailored toward the different types of provinces. Frontier provinces would benefit from STI policies that direct increased support toward the already developed value-added productive sectors, especially those that are part of the export basket. For example, two frontier provinces—Jujuy and Santa Fe—both export more products, more volume, and more sophisticated goods than other provinces. STI policies in Santa Fe could provide specialized support to businesses in the agroindustrial sector related to the national quality infrastructure or other more advanced hurdles. Since these types of provinces tend to have a relatively sophisticated productive sector, further support for the existing components of the ecosystem (for example, incubators and accelerators) could result in an even stronger STI ecosystem.

Emerging regions with considerably fewer innovation actors would benefit from STI policies that enable knowledge transfer from frontier provinces, ideally targeting high-potential sectors. Emerging regions are generally characterized by sprouts of innovation led by driven entrepreneurs with access to finance and networks. By targeting STI policies at the sectors associated with these innovation sprouts, STI policy can capitalize on the momentum that already exists to spur further innovation.

Improving public sector capacity is also of key importance for helping emerging regions to catch up with frontier and more central regions, along with fully benefiting from the national innovation system. Local governments have an important role to play as providers of funds and designers of innovation programs, along with being *brokers of federal programs.* These authorities can help to identify opportunities and support local entrepreneurs in navigating the ecosystem, including accessing national programs.

Across different types of regions, natural resources with a comparative advantage provide an opportunity to kick-start new innovative sectors. For example, innovative ventures in Jujuy include new enterprises in the lithium sector that build on newly discovered mineral ventures. Innovations in archeology build on the Incan historic ruins in the region, along with new enterprises that incorporate digital technologies in the tourism sector and leverage the region's cultural heritage. Because of the yearlong sunlight, the region is also developing a new solar power and alternative energy sector. Private sector enterprises, such as Fundación Ecoandina, are developing capabilities in local communities to use solar energy in engineering, infrastructure, and cooking. The foundation was created by German immigrants with some knowledge of solar power and is facilitating technology transfer between Germany and Jujuy Province.

Regions with a history of STI in specific sectors provide a comparative advantage for new opportunities and innovative sectors. Neuquén is an interesting example of a province with frontier sectors, but little interaction between the top research sectors and the productive sector. Each project is large, with nuclear, satellite, and space industries overrepresented. STI policies that target support at this sector would likely be most effective there.

Increasing convergence and catch-up require shifting innovation policy from knowledge production to knowledge diffusion and adoption. The heterogeneity of experiences in Argentina over the past 10 years and the persistent heterogeneity in regional productive and innovative performance require policies that create and support local public and private sector capabilities to identify and use the assets of the national innovation system.

APPENDIX B

Evolution of CONICET and Estación Experimental Obispo Colombres

CASE STUDY 1. SUPPLY SIDE (KNOWLEDGE GENERATION): CONICET TECNOLOGÍAS

The National Science and Technical Research Council (CONICET) is the main science and technology institution in Argentina, with more than 10,000 full-time researchers and agreements with the main universities and other science and technology organizations across the country. CONICET was established in 1958 by Nobel Prize winner Bernardo Houssay with the aim of creating an enclave of academic excellence.

While the organization's mission was traditionally oriented toward research published in peer-review publications, CONICET Tecnologías (the management unit of Technology Transfer) was created within the last decade. Since 2017, this unit has been the management office of CONICET and is responsible for knowledge transfer from CONICET researchers to society at-large.

At that time, CONICET reoriented its focus to finding users (both current and potential) for its knowledge. It began by taking an inventory of what its researchers create and marketing that knowledge. The process of cataloging research inventories is essentially one of self-discovery for the organization.

Organization of CONICET Tecnologías and its technology transfer instruments

CONICET Tecnologías is organized in three thematic areas: (a) health, food, and biotech (which represent the main competitive advantages of Argentina); (b) engineering, environment, and energy; and (c) sustainable and inclusive development (which encompasses the work with public and social sectors). The three units promote technology transfer both within CONICET and with external clients. CONICET Tecnologías also oversees licensing and patent applications.

The INNOVA-T Foundation is an important component not currently reflected in CONICET's organizational chart. It plays a critical role by channeling all revenues from technology transfer. CONICET Tecnologías generates business and delivers services, while INNOVA-T administers revenues from these services.

CONICET Tecnologías has three technology transfer instruments.

Technology transfer offices at the provincial level

Each management unit at a provincial level has a technology transfer office. There are 17 technology transfer offices in Argentina.

New evaluation and information system

To develop science and technology knowledge, CONICET gives special importance to the selection, training, evaluation, and promotion of its research staff. For example, in their Management and Evaluation System, the scientific output of researchers is given as much weight as technological developments or technology transfer activities.

Problem-solving networks as business development tools and coordination devices

Problem-solving networks are associations of researchers or research groups (internal to CONICET or from other science and technology organizations) and public or private stakeholders. They facilitate collective action to integrate capabilities and find solutions to specific problems of a comprehensive nature. Networks have a medium- and long-term work horizon according to the problems to be addressed.

Main indicators of performance

The primary indicators for CONICET's technology transfer achievements are technological production, technology-based enterprises, technological and social development, and enabled cognitive services.

Technological production

CONICET submits the largest number of annual patent applications to the National Institute of Industrial Property of Argentina. In 2017, CONICET requested 75 patents worldwide, of which 33 were new inventions. For the past four years, the number of patent requests was even higher, above 80 per year; of these, two industrial design patents and six software patents were registered. The transfer of technology from CONICET to the socioproductive sector is enabled through a licensing process, with five licenses issued in 2017. CONICET manages 21 research and development (R&D) projects with the socioproductive sector that, in the future, may represent new technologies to be protected or licensed.

Technology-based enterprises

Technology-based companies aim to exploit new products or services based on scientific and technological research results. To form a technology-based company, researchers and CONICET professionals work together with entrepreneurs and institutional and private investors. In all, 28 technology-based companies have been constituted, 6 of them in 2017.

Technological and social development projects

CONICET works with the Ministry of Science, Technology, and Productive Innovation (MINCyT) through a program called Technological and Social Development Projects, which seeks to solve a market or social need in which one or more organizations (public or private) are a technology. The organizations must have financing from one or more institutions; CONICET provides human resources to develop the technology. In 2016, 93 projects qualified for financing; 19 projects qualified in 2017.

Enabled cognitive services

Cognitive services are carried out by highly qualified professionals who use a specific scientific-technological knowledge for the analysis, evaluation, and generation of proposals to improve products, organizations, or processes. Cognitive services also include the application of procedures and the use of state-of-the-art technological instruments. In 2017, 537 high-level technological services and 105 advisory services were implemented, and 16 technical assistance agreements were signed.

National Science and Justice Program

The National Science and Justice Program aims to strengthen ties between the scientific community and judicial authorities throughout the country to bring forensic science to society. CONICET has offered its research, equipment, and training capabilities for years to provide solutions to the specific needs of judges and prosecutors. This program promotes the operational links between CONICET and the judiciary.

Programs and activities of "sticky people"

CONICET Tecnologías was developed in response to the emerging collaborative economy, not only in Argentina but globally, where open innovation is the rule. CONICET Tecnologías was intended to build stronger linkages with industry and to reorient its scientific excellence toward the needs of the private sector in Argentina.

For that reason, this "double-agent" promoter of technology transfer needs to have an entrepreneurial attitude: it needs to be proactive and creative in helping scientists engage with the rest of the world. The concept of "sticky people"—a group of individuals who stick around and stick together—is central in defining the reality of bridge organizations like CONICET Tecnologías. Sticky people are characterized by the 3Ps: patience, perseverance, and persistence. When confronted with important challenges, they display entrepreneurial qualities on three fronts: with skeptical CONICET researchers, they advocate for what is possible; with doubtful customers from the productive sector, they advocate for their products and services; and within highly fragmented innovation systems, they break down institutional silos. Sticky people are central to CONICET's technology transfer.

CONICET itself is a good illustration of this thesis. In 1958, Bernardo Houssay created an exclave in CONICET—a micro environment—for a group of sticky people to do world-class science.

The main issue for CONICET Tecnologías now is to provide a micro environment for the programs that sticky people create. Such programs and activities should become the cost center in an immediate perspective, a profit center in a short-term horizon, and eventually a CONICET Tecnologías spin-off as an independent and autonomous organization.

Way forward in the immediate, short, and medium terms

As of June 2018, CONICET Tecnologías had about 75 professionals: 45 in the central office in Buenos Aires and about 30 in provincial units. CONICET Tecnologías faces several challenges, especially regarding its employees.

The first challenge is a substantial brain drain: many talented professionals are leaving Argentina, particularly those trained abroad. For example, few of the CONICET lawyers trained at the University of California Los Angeles, technology-related employees trained at Oxford University, and social sciences employees trained at the Spanish National Research Council remain at CONICET.

Additionally, budget cuts, which are part of economywide fiscal adjustments, make it hard to fill vacant positions and lead to high staff turnover. Growing demand for technology transfer professionals in the private sector and in universities is another reason: salaries in the private sector are generally higher than CONICET can offer.

As their personal professional agenda evolves, sticky people tend to change positions. They have their own views and agendas and do not fit easily within established hierarchies. They are like flowing water: indispensable but difficult to keep in a single company. CONICET Tecnologías is likely to lose its best and brightest, even under conditions of better budget stability and relatively high salaries.

Therefore, this situation poses two challenges: first, how to retain such individuals within the organization and, second, how to maintain links with them once they have left. There are two routes to address the loss of talent both at present and under the best of circumstances. To start with, some immediate measures, such as the creation of cost centers for the most successful and visible CONICET Tecnologías programs, could be taken to kick-start this medium-term program of organizational transformation. In the medium term, CONICET Tecnologías could be reconstituted as a spin-off of CONICET, private in form but public in purpose. This spin-off would have to be able to generate revenues from technology transfer activities to cover part of operational costs. In a more general sense, it should articulate success stories of technology transfer and commercialization and make them known to society.

Finding quick wins is essential—that is, it is essential to find what is already dynamic and moving and to rely on these segments to accomplish the proposed objectives. An entry point could be the association of CONICET with dynamic technology transfer organizations, such as INIS Biotech, the technology transfer arm of the Leloir Institute. INIS Biotech is currently small, but it is dynamic and expanding, with high growth potential given the excellence of the Leloir Institute. With time, this partnership could become an organizational platform for a CONICET Tecnologías spin-off.

Also in the medium term, creation of a national alliance of technology transfer and commercialization professionals or CONICET Tecnologías alumni network should be considered. Efforts could begin with the city and province of Buenos Aires, Santa Fe (Bariloche and Rosario), and Córdoba, the three locations where informal networks of technology transfer sticky people are already active. As these three locations demonstrate success in a broad sense, other provincial networks can be created or these initial three can be expanded into other provinces. The alumni association of the G-TEC program already exists and could be leveraged as a starting point.[1] Each provincial association can have a governing body, regular meeting schedule, and other knowledge-sharing activities. With time, as these regional associations show results, they can grow into a national one.

CASE STUDY 2. DEMAND SIDE (KNOWLEDGE ADOPTION): ESTACIÓN EXPERIMENTAL (EEAOC) IN TUCUMÁN

Tucumán is the smallest province of Argentina. Industrialization in Tucumán started with processing and transporting sugarcane to the port of Buenos Aires more than a century ago. Provincial gross domestic product (GDP) is just over 50 percent of national per capita GDP, yet the province has two unusual institutional assets. Known as the Garden of the Republic, Tucumán is Argentina's largest producer of lemons and lemon varieties in the world, with Spain as the main buyer. This accomplishment is even more impressive because lemon exports are a recent phenomenon: within the last 40 years, the Estación Experimental Agroindustrial Obispo Colombres—Experimental Agroindustrial Station Obispo Colombres (EEAOC, for its acronym in Spanish)—developed genetic varieties of lemon and infrastructure to ensure compliance with strict European and American phytosanitary standards.

Founded in 1909 by the visionary leader Alejandro Guzmán and funded largely by the association of sugarcane producers, EEAOC introduced a genetic variety of soya on a large scale in the 1970s and 1980. Before that, soya had been cultivated on a limited basis. The introduction and continuous improvement of three commercial export crops—sugarcane, lemons (and other citrus), and soya—in Argentina makes EEAOC a paragon of self-discovery.

Organization of EEAOC

EEAOC is an organization of applied research in plant breeding, plant health, fertilization, agricultural machinery, and industrial processing. It investigates and develops sugarcane, cereals, forage crops, fiber and oilseed crops, fruits and vegetables, medicinal and aromatic plants, and various forest tree species. The main station sits on 85 hectares, with four substations located in distinct agroecological zones of the province.

An ad honorem directory of 10 members manages the EEAOC. These members represent the main productive and agroindustry sectors of Tucumán and are appointed every four years by the executive power of the province. The organizational structure focuses on research, technology transfer, and services. Currently EEAOC supports five programs (sugarcane, citrus, grains, industrialization of sugarcane, and bioenergy) and nine independent projects (usually smaller than the programs).

The internal rate of return for the three main products of EEAOC is high. Between 1960 and 2009, for each peso invested in R&D and extension of those crops, the internal rate of return was 25.33 percent for sugar, 20.54 percent for soya, and 29.35 percent for lemons. However, these numbers measure the effects only in Tucumán and do not capture externalities beyond the province.

Most EEAOC revenue comes from levies for services (taxes) from agricultural producers and customers (70 percent), with about 15 percent from intellectual property (such as licensing and royalties) and other services and products, and the remaining 15 percent from provincial government contributions, subsidies for specific projects, and an honorary pension from MINCyT. Provincial government support acts as a shock absorber, covering 10 percent to 20 percent of the costs in years with poor returns (for instance, when there is a drought), but providing negligible contributions in years with good harvest. Therefore, EEAOC's financial viability depends on its ability to prove value to the private sector.

First-mover role

EEAOC's main role is as a "first-mover plus," meaning that it both sets an example for private producers to follow and helps them to emulate its good practices and become profitable. This triggers a virtuous circle of growth among its clients, both private and public.

Since most social returns are externalities, calculating the aggregate social return for first-mover activities is difficult. Worth highlighting, though, is that the EEAOC's role is not so much introducing genetic varieties of new crops, but introducing new collaborative phytosanitary and quality standards.

Toyota-style continuous Improvement

EEAOC's success is likely due to a rigorous Toyota-style process of continuous improvement for its main crops from Tucumán and the Northwest region.[2] The early detection of problems and the introduction and continuous improvement of new products are the result of close collaboration with agricultural producers.

Problems are detected early through regular meetings of EEAOC's staff with agricultural producers and associations in which they are organized. The 10-member directory has representatives of all major agricultural producers, making continuous feedback smooth and timely. Early detection implies focusing on the prevention of problems, rather than on their resolution.

Sugarcane provides a good example. The sugarcane program has two subprograms: (a) the Genetic Improvement Program, which creates and introduces new varieties with increasing yields of sucrose, ethanol, and biomass per area unit, and (b) the Agroindustry Program, aimed at improving crop management and assuring early detection of problems by monitoring weeds, diseases, and pests. The agroindustry subprogram has generated the Probicaña (Bicentennial Program of the Sugarcane), which creates a technological package for cultivating sugarcane through new designs for planting and irrigation, innovative developments in agricultural machinery, and other techniques to improve the productivity and sustainability of the sugarcane area. This technological package is delivered to producers by a private firm (Zafra SA, representative of the American firm John Deere) under an agreement in which the EEAOC receives royalties from Zafra.

EEAOC's dilemma and options to resolve it

Each of the three products that Tucumán Province has introduced in Argentina have also been introduced to the rest of the world. Lemon 2.0, soya 2.0, and sugarcane 2.0 have been sufficiently refined to lose some of their commodity-like characteristics: the number and value of derivatives of the original products are virtually limitless, but to be able to develop products and satisfy the requirements of global markets, collaboration with other research organizations and future customers is a must. Recognizing this emerging reality, EEAOC and CONICET created a joint venture in 2013: the Institute of Agribusiness Technology of the Argentine Northwest.

The government of Tucumán Province does not define and fund EEAOC's priorities and activities; rather, the board of directors, which consists of private sector representatives, do so. The organization is efficient, yet it must become a platform for collaboration. To be able to develop and derive value from agricultural products 2.0, a key recommendation is for EEAOC to generate a spin-off; a joint venture between the main knowledge players in the Northeast region. Such a spin-off will become a platform for a small number of collaborative strategic bets—that is to say, a small number of user-driven long-term innovation consortiums.

Densely populated with research and innovation organizations, Tucumán has networks that link their leaders with leaders in the government and private sector. These networks are crucial assets for a collaborative economy. One of the common characteristics of successful innovation systems is the presence of close long-term relationships between individuals who work consistently together to accelerate development. These relationships typically extend beyond the boundaries of a single institution. Over time, sticky people operate between institutions, carrying their networks with them.

The economy of Tucumán has created two generations of sticky people. The first generation was structured at the turn of the 20th century around the founding fathers of two key knowledge institutions: EEAOC and the National University of Tucumán. The second generation, from the beginning of the 1970s up to now, created the current knowledge institutions of the province.

Members of this second generation have now retired or are close to retirement, and the network has lost some of its dynamism. Maturation of networks of change makers is by no means a phenomenon specific to Tucumán. A common solution is to look at the diaspora of high achievers in Argentina and the world. Diaspora high achievers have two characteristics: (1) they have achieved exceptional status in the profession and would bring this status to their home locality, rather than seeking to enhance their status from it, and (2) they are exploring new horizons and opportunities in life. For such high achievers, returning to Tucumán for a new professional challenge can be an attractive possibility.

Tucumán and EEAOC as entry points of national self-discovery

EEAOC is a model of a trial-and-error process of discovery of new products to export and new patterns of regional specialization. It is a rare example of the so-called Schumpeterian Development Agency (SDA), an agency capable of accountable experimentation. Capabilities and motivation to experiment (to make mistakes and correct them) does not come easily for the public sector, and this is why such organizations are unique in the world. The fact that a successful SDA has existed for more than 100 years in Argentina, having survived the country's numerous macroeconomic and institutional shocks, is truly remarkable. It is a testimony not just to the efficacy of its private sector – and demand-driven organizational model (the organization lives from the dues of private sector associations and from the sale of services to the private sector), but also to the vitality and dynamism of Argentina as a country.

So why are SDAs so crucial, and should Argentina have more of them? As it stands, the future is open-ended, with no ready benchmarks. However, it is probable that in the future, commodities will be transformed into customized knowledge-based products. What the future will have needs to be discovered through collaborative large-scale innovation projects called strategic bets. Crisis is usually the time to trigger self-discovery. Argentina can construct its own specific portfolio of strategic bets and test its vision of a knowledge-based future. The country has assets that can trigger such self-discovery, but it needs a sense of urgency to define the opportunities of the future.

NOTES

1. G-TEC is a graduate program of specialization in technology management, innovation, and technology transfer carried out by a consortium of institutions from the academic world and the productive sector. It depends on MINCyT through FONARSEC (the National Agency for Scientific and Technological Promotion).
2. The Toyota Way is a set of principles and behaviors that underlie the Toyota Motor Corporation's managerial approach and production system. First articulated in 2001, it consists of principles in two key areas: continuous improvement and respect for people.

REFERENCE

CONICET (National Science and Technical Research Council). 2018. "Indicadores: Vinculación y producción tecnológica." CONICET, Buenos Aires.

APPENDIX C

Innovation per Methodology: Quality of the Policy Mix Analysis

This appendix provides guidance to practitioners embarking on an analysis of the quality of the policy mix in cases where the public expenditure review (PER) focuses on science, technology, and innovation (STI) only or on business support policies more generally.

This task has two objectives:

- To assess the internal consistency of resource allocation for each instrument, including size, scale effects, and redundancies, and the alignment between policy objectives and outcomes, department mandates, instruments used, and types of beneficiaries
- To evaluate the coherence between the country's priorities and the composition of the portfolio of instruments (policy mix).

The framework compares the policy priorities for innovation with the set of policy instruments. At the core, the analysis transitions the focus from descriptive to prescriptive analytics by evaluating the coherence between priorities and the portfolio and by assessing the internal consistency of the policy mix. Since the policy portfolio tends to grow organically, it is common to find some degree of fragmentation, overlapping policies, and legacy programs that are ready for rationalization.

The overview of the analytical framework in figure C.1 depicts the general approach and presents three components: (1) country needs assessments, (2) policy mapping, and (3) coherence and consistency of the analysis. The country needs assessments and the policy mapping are necessary inputs for the analysis of coherence and consistency (that is, they should be undertaken prior to the portfolio analysis). The framework states that policy priorities are a function of unmet needs for policy support and the strategic policy aspirations as stated by policy makers. The information for analyzing the portfolio of instruments comes predominantly from the policy mapping exercise. The ability to articulate recommendations (that is, make value judgments) regarding the adequacy of the composition of the policy mix rests on an understanding of the country's context and implicit or explicit priorities.

FIGURE C.1
Framework overview

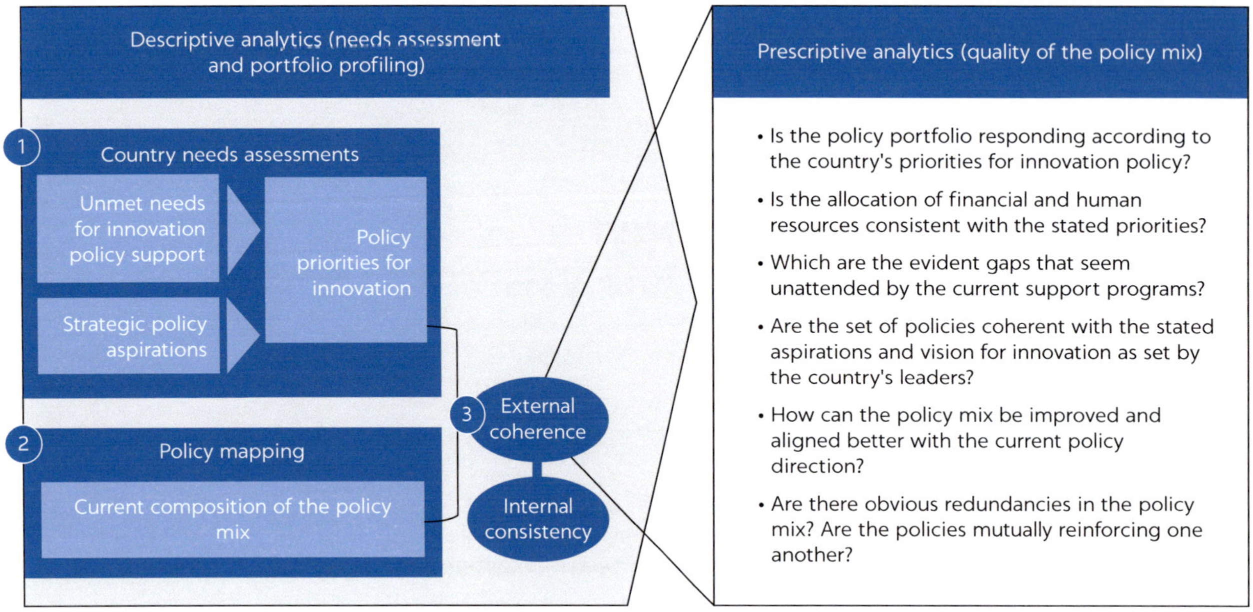

Source: World Bank 2019.

This appendix discusses the country needs assessments and policy mapping, with an eye to consistency and coherence of the analysis.

COUNTRY NEEDS ASSESSMENTS

The PER evaluates the policy mix by analyzing the patterns of public spending in STI and the way in which resources are allocated. A sensible way to assess whether this spending is appropriate for the country is to understand the country's context. For example, what is the case for advancing STI policy in the country? Are the country's firms, academic institutions, and other stakeholders producing the desired outcomes? Why do we believe that they are performing the way they do? (And how do we know?) How conducive are local conditions to desired outcomes? Who are the main stakeholders in the national innovation system (NIS)? How are they supposed to contribute to the desired outcomes delivered by the policy mix? Is the institutional framework for business growth and innovation adequate? What national policy strategies and programs have led to the current policy mix? What are the main challenges and opportunities to advancing the desired outcomes? What policy support needed by business and other NIS actors appears to be unmet? Which segment of firms seem to have experienced lower innovation performance?

Goals

The country needs assessment has four goals:

- Understand the country's needs for STI or business support policies and the developmental challenges linked to achieving its desired results.

- Evaluate whether these needs are reflected in the strategic policy priorities.
- Identify the needs for further policy support and opportunities to rationalize the policy mix.
- Identify unnecessary overlaps in policies and between institutions that will lead to a more efficient and coordinated policy mix.

As a result of the country needs assessment, the task team produces a country inception report, which should contain at least, the following:

- A relative comparison (benchmark) of the country's performance (outcomes), such as productivity growth, export performance, competitiveness indicators, and diversification measures, and its NIS in relation to that of its peers
- A review of the strategic context of innovation or business support policy, including an assessment of existing conditions and barriers for knowledge accumulation (human capital, infrastructure) and the prevalent incentives for firms to accumulate knowledge and become more productive and competitive
- An assessment of behavioral patterns of firms in acquiring capabilities, including investments in research and development (R&D) and non-R&D innovation, competencies, and technology
- An overview of the institutional framework, policies, programs, and policy mix.

Approach

The analytical framework used to assess the country's needs compares the underlying demand for STI or business support policy with the existing policy framework and provision of support in the form of policies and programs. The analysis sheds light on how consistently the country's existing policies and programs respond to that demand. The observed gaps (if any) enable clients to identify possible steps toward bridging them.

The approach for this analysis recognizes that not all of the observed parameters remain under the control of the policy makers; as such, many determinants of demand are exogenous variables, such as external competitive pressures, the business environment broadly defined, and other contextual macroeconomic variables, such as interest rates. More specifically, the following are key features of the proposed framework:

- Assumes that STI policy priorities are a function of developmental challenges (that is, technical opportunity)
- Assesses how consistently the country's policy programs respond to the identified developmental challenges
- Assumes that policy programs can affect STI and other business-related outcomes
- Recognizes that not all variables affecting outcomes fall within the control of the policy maker
- Provides a high-level overview of the policy programs and allocated resources.

Detailed analysis is delivered at subsequent stages of the engagement. The country needs assessment provides a general overview of the policy instrument and a description of the program. A detailed analysis of the policy portfolio mapping that contains a conclusion about the quality of the policy mix and a detailed description of resource allocation and trends is under the scope of a different module. Figure C.2 provides an overview of the analytical framework.

FIGURE C.2

Approach to assessing policy priorities for innovation

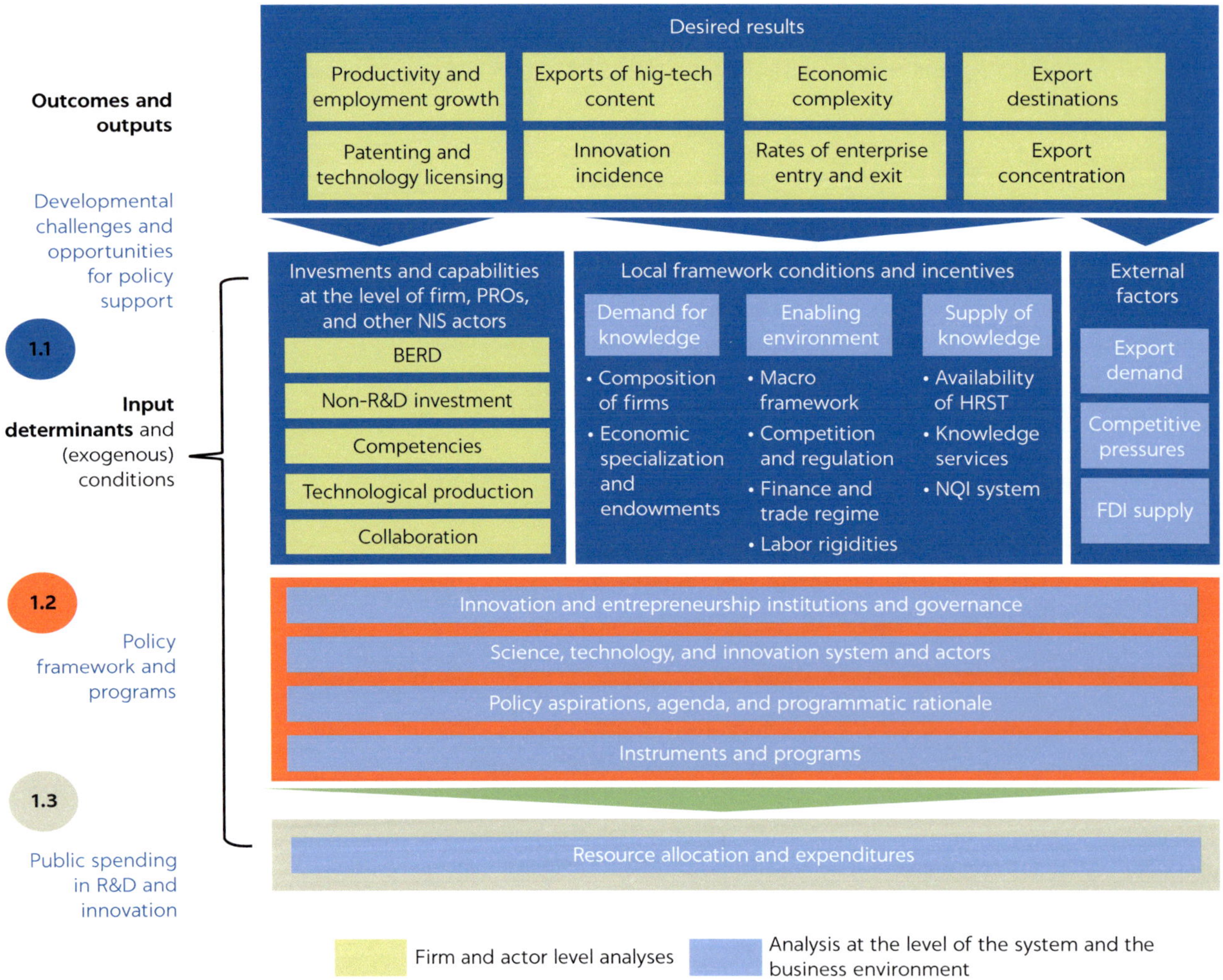

Source: World Bank 2019.
Note: BERD = business expenditure on R&D; FDI = foreign direct investment; HRST = human resources, science, and technology; NIS = national innovation system; NQI = national quality infrastructure; PROs = public research organizations; R&D = research and development.

Scope

A critical element in the public expenditure review analysis is the definition of the scope of policies—STI policies, small and medium enterprise (SME) policies, or business support policies more generally. This is the first element to be agreed with the client. For example, in the case of STI, where should the line be drawn for science—PhD grants, research excellence, or somewhere else?—and for innovation—R&D, upgrading programs, or supplier development programs? In the case of innovation, it is important to use a broader definition that includes any improvement in products, processes, technology, business models, or managerial and organizational practices. If the focus is on SMEs, similar decisions need to be made for more sector-specific policies that, although not directly targeting SMEs, also include SMEs.

Several additional features are related to the scope of the work:

- *Multilevel analysis*, which includes assessment of parameters at the level of the firm (that is, prevalence of innovation) and at the level of the national innovation system or ecosystem (that is, factor conditions)
- *Benchmarking*, which is when the scope of work assesses comparative performance and compares existing conditions in the country to those of structural and regional peers; for example, the PER conducted in Chile selected Australia, Canada, and Norway as the country's structural peers based on the following characteristics: (a) they are high-income Organisation for Economic Co-operation and Development (OECD) countries, (b) natural resources constitute more than 30 percent of their exports, (c) their population is greater than 5 million, and (d) they own a sovereign wealth fund
- *Subnational analysis*, which examines differences in performance and demand for policies across regions in the country.

Methodology for data collection

The country needs assessment uses primary and secondary sources of data to produce information. Innovation policy analysis can be carried out on primary and secondary sources of data. Secondary sources mostly entail databases that compare countries and ecosystems at the aggregate, such as the conference board for aggregate productivity metrics or the OECD innovation indicators when suitable. Trade-related performance data can be found in World Bank World Development Indicators (World Bank 2017) or in United Nations COMTRADE (United Nations, various years). Information regarding local framework conditions usually resides in country-specialized publications and reports, such as the OECD reviews for innovation policy, and in country-featured monitoring indicators, such as the Global Entrepreneurship Monitor consortium. The analysis can also include semi-structured interviews with key informants and topic experts.

By way of comparison with similar frameworks, the country's needs assessment is usually sector agnostic (that is, it does not have a vertical focus, as in a digital ecosystem analysis) and does not include culture and attitudes as a domain for analysis. It does not focus exclusively on early-stage firms (tech start-up ecosystem analysis) or focus on assessing the density of the start-up community (tech start-up ecosystem analysis).

In terms of the contrasts related to analytics and methodology for data collection, the country needs assessment usually does not conduct either quantitative surveys or focus group discussions (that is, a digital ecosystem analysis) or collect extensive data on start-up founders (that is, a tech start-up ecosystem analysis).

COMPOSITION OF THE POLICY MIX

This analytical component builds the profile of the policy mix. At its core, the exercise helps practitioners to populate the matrix for policy mapping.

Goals

There are two main goals:

- Collect the data for mapping the portfolio of programs.
- Provide the basis for running descriptive analytics and for profiling the portfolio.

The expected results from the data collection exercise include a database of the portfolio for the specified parameters of interest and a descriptive profile of the instrument portfolio and policy mix.

More broadly, the policy map provides a representation of the innovation policy budget structure and its allocation by intermediate outcomes. With this profile, the team can assess the internal consistency of instruments in terms of resource allocation—size, scale effects, and redundancies—and the alignment between policy objectives or outcomes, departments' mandates, instruments used, and types of beneficiaries; the team can also evaluate the coherence between the demand for innovation (country's needs) and the composition of the portfolio of instruments or policy mix. The matrix can also help the team to build a profile of spending in SME and innovation policy and the flow of funds of organizations and programs (how much is spent, by whom, and for what objective) and to assess the consistency and coherence of the policy mix in relation to the country's needs and demand for policy.

TABLE C.1 **Category description of profiling parameters**

CATEGORY	DEFINITION	OBJECTIVE	VARIABLES[a]
General information	Instrument identification and dependency	Identify budget allocation, agencies or department roles, overlaps, budget concentration, and capacities concentration	Project identification, ministry or institution, directorate, department, agency, and so forth
Economy or society outcomes	Expected impacts and effects achieved with the instrument; expected results generated in the economy as well as in society	Capture high-level outcome related to policy aspirations to inform the coherence analysis between instrument goals and systemic goals	Productivity, diversification, research excellence, societal development, technology adoption, new markets, human capital, social innovation, start-up behavior, and so forth
Instrument objective	The state or goals the instrument intends to produce	Register the intent behind the policy program to address the specific market failure or identified problem	Research excellence, technology transfer, science-industry collaboration, business R&D, non-R&D innovation, technology adoption, and so forth
Ecosystem	Configured by all key actors, includes rules, supply and demand, as well as strengths and weakness of the innovation and entrepreneurship initiatives	Understand the nature of the instrument and visualize the potential impact in the ecosystem	Capabilities of the ecosystem: institutions, agencies, associations, clusters, and infrastructure Supply of actors: direct or indirect support to enhance capabilities of knowledge providers—researchers, universities, R&D centers Access to innovation and entrepreneurship finance

continued

TABLE C.1 *continued*

CATEGORY	DEFINITION	OBJECTIVE	VARIABLES[a]
Type of support	Government direct R&D funding includes grants, loans, and procurement; government indirect R&D funding includes tax incentives such as R&D tax credits, R&D allowances, reductions in R&D workers' wage taxes and social security contributions, and accelerated depreciation of R&D capital (OECD 2010)	Assess the level of government participation, partnership, and implementation around the different types of instruments	Direct or indirect; each country would have its own strategy to promote innovation
Mechanism of intervention	Type of instruments or actions used to deliver and implement the program	Categorize the tools and mechanisms used to deliver a pool of programs to analyze their suitability to the needs	Grants, vouchers for innovation and collaboration, tax incentives, early-stage infrastructure, scholarship, advisory, credit, and so forth
Cofinancing	Support given through a subsidy—for example, a matching grant for business R&D or a subsidy for technical consulting	Assess joint efforts to promote and enhance STI programs	Subsidy for the business sector; the matching contribution from the beneficiary can be in cash or in kind
Grant usage	Purpose and destination of the resources under the grant category	Assess the portfolio mix of instruments and value the different lines of support	Market research, space and rent, business operation, promotion and marketing, and so forth
Sector orientation	Where the instruments or programs are directed: cross-sectoral or targeted to specific niches	Distinguish concentration or prioritization efforts	Vertical-sector orientation, horizontal
Geographic coverage	Scope of application of the instrument and where the intended beneficiaries lie on the map	Understand the breadth of application of the instrument	National, regional, and provincial instruments
Sector	Sector where the instrument is targeted	Separate by sector the level of support and instruments available	Agriculture, manufacturing, mining, tourism, forestry, construction, fishing, technology, education, health services, finance, retail, transportation, entertainment, and so forth
Beneficiaries	Group of people or institutions that the program is targeting	Map the different groups who are receiving any type of funding or support	Private sector, nongovernmental organizations, universities, start-ups, and so forth
Life cycle	Which phase of the business is being targeted for support (applies for business ventures)	Map the various types of support along the different stages of the business	Seed and pre-seed, young start-up, scale-up, mature
Size	Range of revenue generated by the companies supported	Measure the proportion of support for each group	Micro, small, medium, large[b]
Innovation propensity of the beneficiary	Which innovation stage is being supported	Acknowledge the level of engagement and support around innovation	Noninnovator, potential innovator, innovator
Budget	Revision of different years, ideally last three years	Compare and recognize trends, changes of strategies, and commitment through time	Years analysis
Budget source	Where does the money come from: account name or department glossary	Identify the different level of support and funding inputs	Source of funding

Source: World Bank.
Note: R&D = research and development; STI = science, technology, and innovation.
a. The metrics are often a dummy variable, 0 or 1, to indicate the presence or absence of each variable. Percentages may be used to denote the level of action or presence in a variable. In addition, overlaps and redundancies can be registered as well.
b. According to the World Bank enterprise surveys, the size of companies is defined by the number employees: fewer than 5 (micro), 19 (small), 20–99 (medium), 100+ (large).

Approach

The portfolio mapping provides the basis for coherence and consistency analysis as part of the review of the quality of the policy mix. The accompanying data collection tool provides the structure for gathering information. The process of entering and surveying data needs to be agreed with the client, and focal points from the implementing agencies should commit to providing the data required. The client usually nominates someone as the main point of contact who assumes responsibility for filling the matrix within the specified time frame.

REFERENCES

OECD (Organisation for Economic Co-operation and Development). 2010. *Measuring Innovation: A New Perspective*. Paris: OECD.

United Nations. Various years. COMTRADE (database). New York: United Nations.

World Bank. 2017. Enterprise Survey (database). Washington, DC: World Bank.

World Bank. 2019. *World Development Report 2019: The Changing Nature of Work*. Washington, DC: World Bank.

APPENDIX D

Conducting a "Light" Innovation PER in Argentina: Data Collection Issues and Strategy

Argentina has a complex mix of policies to support production, innovation, and entrepreneurship. They can be evaluated at different levels of aggregation and for different periods of time. In this appendix, we perform two types of analysis. On the one hand, we explore the current policy mix and recent changes over time at the highest level of disaggregation possible based on data from an "instrument matrix" that we constructed. On the other hand, we perform an analysis of longer-term changes, at higher levels of aggregation based on data from the Open Budget.

ANALYSIS BASED ON THE INSTRUMENT MATRIX

To systematize information about policy support for science, technology, and innovation (STI) in Argentina, we constructed a matrix based on the Registro of Subsidios e Incentivos, a list of all available instruments developed by the Ministry of Production, which we updated with information on the Ministry of Economy's website.[1] We call this the "instruments matrix." The different cells of this matrix include information describing the objectives, beneficiaries, instruments of support, and, when available, the budget for each instrument. These elements were completed manually based on secondary information from public sites, reports, and inputs from different ministries.

We identify instruments at the highest level of disaggregation. For example, FONDEAR (Argentine Economic Development Fund) is a program that includes several instruments (FONDEAR productive investment and work capital, FONDEAR capital contribution, FONDEAR interest rate subsidies, and so forth). FONDEAR aims to facilitate the funding of strategic sectors, regional economies, and technological innovation. The specific instruments target more specific goals such as providing loans for pre- and post-export expenses, giving subsidized credit for working capital and productive investments, giving subsidized credit to small and medium enterprises (SMEs) for working capital, and so forth.

Completing this matrix was challenging for two reasons. First, Argentine statistics are generally poor. Evaluations of policies and programs are either nonexistent or performed with different methodologies, which does not allow comparison across programs or over time. In addition, the information is available at different levels of aggregation and is not consistent.

Second, information on the budget allocated to each instrument is not available for all programs. Argentina's public spending is open and accessible,[2] but the allocation of resources to different areas of bureaucracy is provided on a much more aggregated level than the one in the matrix. For this reason, it is not possible to match information with instruments or programs.

A significant amount of work was devoted to gathering a data set that allows us to explore the main questions of this study.

The analysis in this report is based on a version of the matrix completed through fieldwork conducted by the research team in February 2019. At that point in time, the instruments matrix included qualitative information about 216 active and 55 canceled instruments as well as budget data for 103 of the 216 active instruments.

On active and canceled instruments

The matrix contains information about both active and canceled instruments (figure D.1). Analysis of active versus canceled instruments illustrates changes in policy. However, the canceled instruments for which we have information are not representative of all such instruments. Our main analysis, therefore, focuses mainly on the 216 active instruments. We provide some characterization of canceled instruments, but it should be interpreted with caution.

FIGURE D.1

Active instruments, by ministry

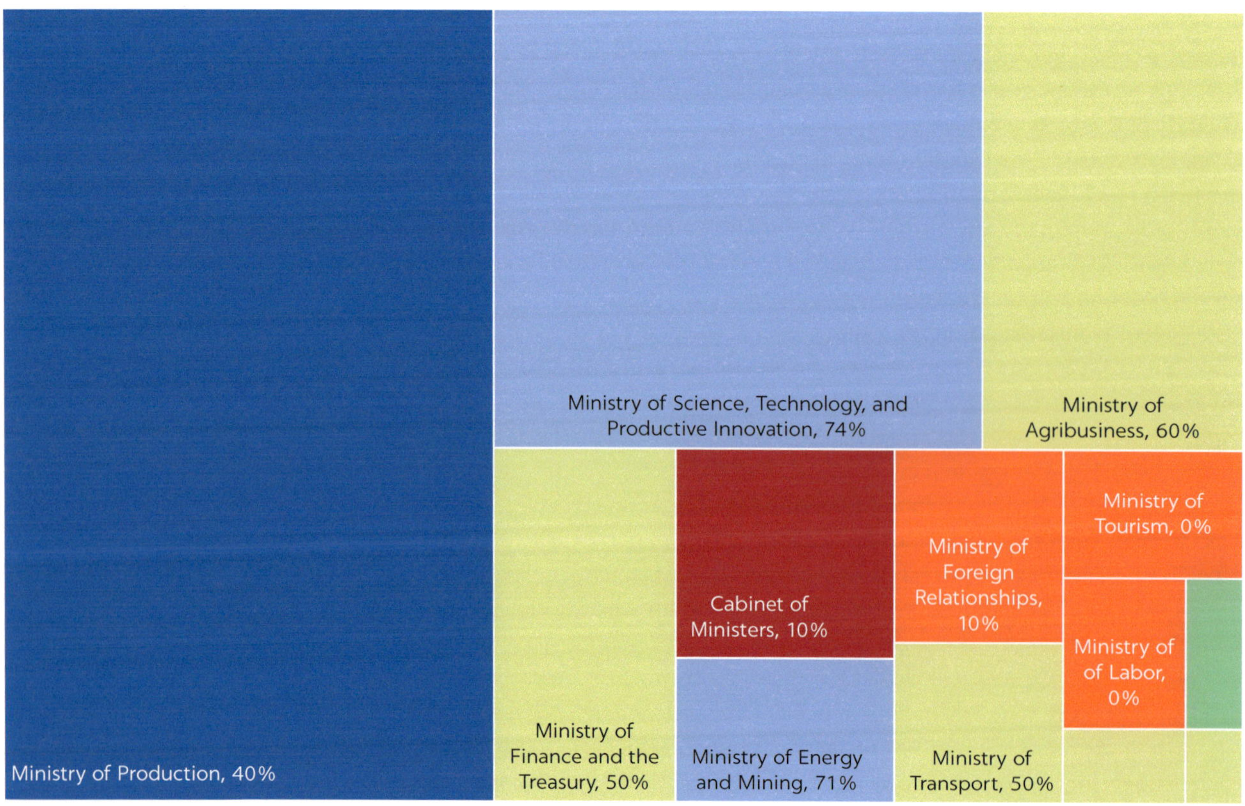

Source: World Bank 2019.

On qualitative and quantitative information in the matrix

Qualitative data about the different instruments were collected based on public information, complemented with interviews. The data on budget, however, are not public and were provided by different departments of government. This second type of data are therefore not only incomplete but also very likely biased, since government departments responded differently to our request for information, and we were unable to identify the reasons why budgetary information was provided in some cases and not in others.

Budget data in the matrix are also difficult to interpret because of the coexistence of different types of support: tax incentives and some kind of disbursement or provision of services or goods (assets or infrastructure, guarantees or public goods). Table D.1 classifies the various instruments included in the matrix according to the main mechanisms of intervention used.

The calculation of efforts or budget allocated to instruments different from tax incentives is straightforward; nevertheless, the funds spent in the form of tax incentives have to be estimated, and this is a complex process that requires a decision regarding the level of economic activity to which the forgone tax should be applied.

We work with official estimates of the budget and funds allocated to instruments that use tax incentives. These estimates are difficult to interpret and compare with the funds oriented to grants because official estimation of tax incentives simply multiplies the observed (ex post) taxable base to the rate of tax reduction—that is, they do not take into account possible changes in behavior induced by the tax incentives. At any point in time, the estimated amount spent on tax incentives is very likely to be overestimated, reflecting the upper bound of the expenditures (it supposes a totally inelastic reaction by economic actors to changes in the tax rates, which is very unlikely). The evolution of these estimates is also difficult to interpret because it captures the combined effect of changes in policies (fewer or greater tax incentives) and changes in economic activity that can be the result of these specific policies or any other factor.

Our main analysis of the current policy mix is therefore based mostly on counts of instruments because this is the most comprehensive and reliable information we have. We use data on budget to show specific points that cannot be evaluated with counts and to illustrate the magnitude in certain cases. We also use data on budget from the matrix to analyze short-term changes in STI.

Analysis of short-term changes in STI cannot be done using counts since we have them for only one year. The instrument matrix, however, allows us to evaluate changes over time, since, when available, budgetary data cover 2012–18. We use these data to explore recent changes in policy, covering 2017–18. This period was chosen for two reasons. First, the matrix includes some canceled instruments for which we do not have information on the budget before its cancellation. Cancellation occurred mainly after the change in administration in 2016–17. We do not have data on instruments that were active in, say, 2012 or 2013 and that are now canceled. Analysis based on the information provided in the matrix on changes over a longer period of time than 2017–18 might be misleading. Second, the data for 2017–18 cover very important changes in policy that this report should capture.

Three types of changes in policy should be captured:

- *Institutional.* One major complication with using these data for long-term analysis has to do with permanent institutional changes that make it difficult

TABLE D.1 **Instruments, by mechanism of intervention**

INSTRUMENT	BRIEF DESCRIPTION	MECHANISM OF INTERVENTION
Business advisory	Services related to advising the private sector on how to improve its current practices	Provision of services or goods
Business education for entrepreneurship	New knowledge created geared for increasing business know-how	Provision of services or goods
Collaborative networks and cluster policy	Geographic concentrations of companies and institutions in a particular field and their collaboration to generate innovation	Provision of services or goods
Credit and loan guarantees for small and medium enterprises (SMEs) and innovation enterprises	Monetary support or guarantees by benefactor if the enterprise or entity fails to achieve its goal	Disbursement
Crowdsourcing and open innovation instruments	Activities seeking to generate innovative ideas, through pooling ideas in an open-source manner and awarding the best ideas	Provision of services or goods
Education and training for entrepreneurship and SMEs	Provision of specialists for various training services geared to SMEs	Provision of services or goods
Equity finance	Funding in exchange for ownership (of a certain percentage) in the enterprise	Disbursement
Grants	Direct allocation of funding from public agencies	Disbursement
Incubators and accelerators	Physical infrastructure catering to start-ups in the earlier stages of their life cycle	Provision of services or goods
Loans and credit	Funds provided to the beneficiary, for which the funds (plus interest) must be paid later	Disbursement
Public goods	Nonrival and nonexcludable goods and services that are accessible to everyone	Provision of services or goods
Public procurement for innovation	Acquisition of technological equipment and machinery by public bodies that enterprises will use for innovation	Provision of services or goods
Quality infrastructure	Public and private parties that deliver specific functions to determine whether a product, process, or service meets a defined set of requirements	Provision of services or goods
Regulatory instruments	Implementation of new public regulation aimed at the program or similar programs	Provision of services or goods
Research infrastructure	Public infrastructure that supports development of quality research for the public or society (for example, public universities)	Provision of services or goods
Scholarships	Awards provided to promising students to study specialization areas of science, technology, and innovation	Disbursement
Science, technology, and industrial parks	Physical infrastructure enclaves providing preferential incentives that support achievement of intended economic goals	Provision of services or goods
Tax incentives	Tax deductions	Tax incentives
Vouchers	Small grants allocated to noninnovative SMEs to purchase services from external knowledge providers	Disbursement

Source: World Bank.

to follow budgets over time for ministries and even more for secretariats. As can be seen in table D.2, the national ministries have changed dramatically since 2007. There were 11 ministries in 2007 and 20 in 2016. In September 2018, 10 ministries were dissolved or merged, so the number of ministries again declined to 10, but their organization was different than in 2007. Longer-term analysis is fairly impossible. The ministries that remain are the Ministry of Economy, the Ministry of Education, Culture, Science, and Technology (called Ministry of STI in our analysis), the Ministry of Production and Labor (called Ministry of Production in our analysis), the Ministry of Health and Social Development, the Ministry of Defense, the Ministry of Transport, the Ministry of Security, the Ministry of the Interior, the Ministry of Justice, the Ministry of External Relations, and the Chief of Cabinet. The ministries that were transformed into secretaries are the Ministry of Environment and Sustainable Development, Ministry of Energy, Ministry of Tourism, Ministry of Labor, Ministry of Health, Ministry of Culture, Ministry of Agribusiness, and Ministry of Science and Technology. Both the Ministry of Agribusiness and the Ministry of Science and Technology are referred to as ministries in our analysis.

- *Strategic.* The main mechanisms of intervention change in form from direct grants to tax incentives in many cases.
- *Magnitude.* There were significant reductions in the budget oriented to support STI. Missing data could play a role in overestimating these cuts. However, even accounting for the missing data in the most conservative way, the reductions are still significant.[3]

Longer-term changes

Changes over a longer period of time are analyzed using data from the Presupuesto Abierto (Open Budget).[4] To perform this analysis, we use three main dimensions presented in the Open Budget: jurisdiction, purpose, and item.

Jurisdiction

The budget is organized according to the ministerial structure, which is the only level that could be followed systematically over time. However, as discussed above, ministries themselves changed (table D.2). We are particularly interested in the areas of production, agribusiness, and science and technology. We analyze three points in time: 2007 (when Open Budget starts), 2015 (change in administration from Cristina Kirchner to Mauricio Macri), and 2018 (last period available). To analyze this evolution, we needed to build comparable jurisdictions, which meant adding information from several ministries whose jurisdiction goes beyond production, agribusiness, and science and technology (for example, education, tourism, finance, and others). However, we analyze the budget oriented to specific purposes and functions, which allows us not to depart too far from our areas of interest: production, agribusiness, and science and technology.

Purpose

This category is divided into social services, economic services, debt services, administration, and defense and security. We are particularly interested in social and economic services. Each purpose is divided into "functions." In social

TABLE D.2 **Changes in Kirchners' and Macri's cabinets, 2007–18**

NÈSTOR KIRCHNER	CRISTINA KIRCHNER	CRISTINA KIRCHNER	MAURICIO MACRI	MAURICIO MACRI	MAURICIO MACRI
2003–07	2007–11	2011–15	2016	2017	2018–19
Ministries: 10	Ministries: 15	Ministries: 16	Ministries: 20	Ministries: 20	Ministries: 10
Ministry of Interior	Ministry of Interior	Ministry of Interior and Transport	Ministry of Interior, Public Works, and Housing	Ministry of Interior, Public Works, and Housing	Ministry of Interior, Public Works, and Housing
Ministry of Foreign Relationships, International Trade, and Religious Affairs	Ministry of Foreign Relationships, International Trade, and Religious Affairs	Ministry of Foreign Relationships and Religious Affairs	Ministry of Foreign Relationships and Religious Affairs	Ministry of Foreign Relationships and Religious Affairs	Ministry of Foreign Relationships and Religious Affairs
Ministry of Justice and Human Rights	Ministry of Justice and Human Rights	Ministry of Justice and Human Rights	Ministry of Justice and Human Rights	Ministry of Justice and Human Rights	Ministry of Justice and Human Rights
Ministry of Homeland Security	Ministry of Homeland Security	Ministry of Homeland Security	Ministry of Homeland Security	Ministry of Homeland Security	Ministry of Homeland Security
Ministry of Defense	Ministry of Defense	Ministry of Defense	Ministry of Defense	Ministry of Defense	Ministry of Defense
Ministry of Economy and Production	Ministry of Economy and Public Finance	Ministry of Economy and Public Finance	Ministry of Treasury and Public Finance	Ministry of Treasury	Ministry of Treasury
				Ministry of Public Finance	(Absorbed by Treasury)
	Ministry of Agriculture and Fishing	Ministry of Agriculture and Fishing	Ministry of Agribusiness	Ministry of Agribusiness	(Absorbed by Production)
	Ministry of Industry	Ministry of Industry	Ministry of Production	Ministry of Production	Ministry of Production and Labor
	Ministry of Tourism	Ministry of Tourism	Ministry of Tourism	Ministry of Tourism	(Absorbed by President's office)
Ministry of Federal Planning, Public Investment, and Services	Ministry of Federal Planning, Public Investment, and Services	Ministry of Federal Planning, Public Investment, and Services	Ministry of Transport	Ministry of Transport	Ministry of Transport
			Ministry of Energy and Mining	Ministry of Energy and Mining	(Absorbed by Treasury)
			Ministry of Communications	(Absorbed by Modernization)	
			Ministry of Modernization	Ministry of Modernization	(Absorbed by Chief of the Cabinet of Ministers)
Ministry of Education, Science, and Technology	Ministry of Education	Ministry of Education	Ministry of Education and Sports	Ministry of Education and Sports	Ministry of Education, Culture, Science, and Technology
	Ministry of Science, Technology, and Productive Innovation	Ministry of Science, Technology, and Productive Innovation	Ministry of Science, Technology, and Productive Innovation	Ministry of Science, Technology, and Productive Innovation	
		Ministry of Culture	Ministry of Culture	Ministry of Culture	
Ministry of Labor and Social Security	Ministry of Labor and Social Security	Ministry of Labor and Social Security	Ministry of Labor and Social Security	Ministry of Labor and Social Security	(Absorbed by Production)
Ministry of Health	Ministry of Health	Ministry of Health	Ministry of Health	Ministry of Health	(Absorbed by Social Development)
Ministry of Social Development	Ministry of Social Development	Ministry of Social Development	Ministry of Social Development	Ministry of Social Development	Ministry of Health and Social Development
			Ministry of Environment and Sustainable Development	Ministry of Environment and Sustainable Development	(Absorbed by President's office)

Source: Kirchners' administrations based on Chudnovsky and Cafarelli 2018, chart 2.

services, the functions are education and culture, health, housing and urbanism, social assistance, science and technology, water and sanitation, and labor. We discuss information for all of these functions, but we focus on science and technology. In economic services, the functions are energy, fuel, and mining; transport; communications; agriculture; industry; commerce, tourism, and other services; ecology and environment; and insurance and finance. We analyze all of these functions, but we sometimes exclude energy, fuel, and mining; transport; and communication to align the analysis better with policies included in the matrix.

Item

The item shows the type of expenditure and is divided into transfers; debt services and reductions of liabilities; personnel; nonpersonnel services; capital goods; consumption goods; financial assets; and other expenditures. We are particularly interested in transfers, since they represent the budget allocated directly to beneficiaries as direct grants. Transfers are expenses that do not have a counterpart in goods or services, are not refundable, and do not have costs for their use; they are granted to the private sector, public sector institutions (provinces, municipalities, and public companies), and the external sector.

Finally, this information cannot be used to complete the missing information in the instruments matrix because it is aggregated at a level different from that of the instrument matrix. However, it can be used to draw a rough estimation of how much of the total budget oriented to STI is covered with the instrument matrix.

The total amount of transfers associated with science and technology, social services, and economic services to agriculture, industry, and services, spent by the ministries from which we collected data, is the best approximation from Open Budget data that we could use to contrast with figures from the instrument matrix. This amount was US$644 million purchasing power parity (PPP) in 2018 according to Open Budget, and US$198 million PPP, as collected in the instrument budget. If we trust this figure as representing the budget actually directed to STI in direct grants, then we collected just one-third of the budget in the STI matrix. This proportion sounds reasonable, since in 2018 we collected budget for 26 percent of the valid instruments identified.

NOTES

1. See the Ministry of Economy's website at https://www.economia.gob.ar/en/.
2. See https://www.presupuestoabierto.gob.ar.
3. We have budget data for some years (in the period 2012–18) for 103 of the 216 active STI instruments identified (48 percent). However, we have budget data for only 73 of the 216 active instruments (34 percent) for 2018. Additionally, 17 of these estimates are tax incentives, which have many issues. If, for these reasons, we exclude tax incentives, we have budget information for 56 instruments (26 percent). For comparison, for 2017 we have budget data for 76 of the 216 active instruments; if we exclude tax incentives, we have budget data for 57 instruments. Therefore, the situation is very similar in terms of percentage of active instruments for which we have budget data. Even when the number of active instruments with budget data is similar for 2017 and 2018, for some instruments, we have a positive budget for 2017 and a zero budget for 2018 (which account for US$202 million purchasing power parity [PPP]); for some instruments, we have a zero budget in 2017 and a positive budget in 2018 (which accounts for US$45 million PPP). We are not certain whether budget data for these cases are correct or data are missing. The decrease in the

total budget, controlling for inflation, excluding the tax incentives, between 2017 and 2018 was 62 percent (from US$488 million to US$185 million PPP). If we do not take into account the instruments that had zero budget in 2017 or those that had zero budget in 2018, the drop in identified STI expenditure declines to 51 percent (from US$286 million to US$140 million PPP). If we remove only those that did not have a budget in 2018 but did have a budget in 2017, the reduction in expenditure is 35 percent (from US$286 million to US$185 million PPP). This would be a really conservative lower bound estimate of the reduction. PPP dollars are estimated by using the exchange rate resulting from dividing Argentina's 2018 GDP PPP (United Nations Commission for Latin America and Caribbean estimation) by Argentina's preliminary 2018 GDP in Argentine pesos (National Institute of Statistics and Censuses).

4. See https://www.presupuestoabierto.gob.ar.

REFERENCES

Chudnovsky, Mariana, and María Laura Cafarelli. 2018. "Los cambios en las estructuras organizacionales del estado y su vínculo con la composición del empleo público: Argentina, 2003–2016." *Foro Internacional* 58 (2): 275–312. doi:10.24201/fi.v58i2.2465.

World Bank. 2019. *World Development Report 2019: The Changing Nature of Work*. Washington, DC: World Bank.